GLOBETROTTER™

Travel Atlas

SRI LANKA

NEW HOLLAND

New Holland Publishers (UK) Ltd
London • Cape Town • Sydney • Auckland

First edition 2007

10 9 8 7 6 5 4 3 2 1

website:
www.newhollandpublishers.com

Garfield House, 86 Edgware Road
London W2 2EA
United Kingdom

80 McKenzie Street
Cape Town 8001
South Africa

14 Aquatic Drive
Frenchs Forest, NSW 2086
Australia

218 Lake Road
Northcote, Auckland
New Zealand

Distributed in the USA by
The Globe Pequot Press, Connecticut

ISBN 978 1 84537 444 0

Publishing Manager: Thea Grobbelaar
DTP Cartographic Manager: Genené Hart
Editor: Alicha van Reenen
Designers: Genené Hart, Nicole Bannister
Cartographer: Genené Hart
Cartographic Assistants: Tanja Spinola, Reneé Spocter
Picture Research: Shavonne Johannes
Consultant: Lindsay Bennett

Reproduction by Resolution, Cape Town
Printed and bound by Times Offset (M) Sdn. Bhd., Malaysia.

Photographic Credits:
Gerald Cubitt: 17;
Gavin Hellier/jonarnoldimages.com: cover;
Rukshan Jayewardene Photographs: 7, 34 bottom, 40 bottom, 62 top;
Sebastian Posingis: 32 bottom, 34 top, 54 bottom;
Dominic Sansoni: title page, imprint page, 8 top and bottom, 12, 14, 15 top and bottom, 16, 19, 20, 21, 22, 23 top, 25, 28 top and bottom, 30 top, 32 top, 38 top and bottom, 40 top left and top right, 43 top and bottom, 44 bottom, 46 top and bottom, 52 top and bottom, 54 top left and top right, 56 left, 58 top right, 60 bottom, 62 bottom;
Jeroen Snijders: 10, 36 top and bottom, 44 top, 48 bottom, 51, 56 right, 58 top left and bottom, 60 top.

Above: *Sri Lanka's Muslim and Hindu minorities are represented by the green and saffron stripes on the left side of the national flag. There are bo-leaves in each corner.*
Cover: *Tea pickers at a plantation in Talawakele in the Nuwara Eliya Hill Country.*
Title page: *Adam's Peak or Sri Pada is a majestic mountain held to be sacred by all religions on Sri Lanka. At dawn it stands sentinel above the mist caressing the central hills, welcoming the start of the new day.*
Below: *Agriculture and religion are two anchors in the lives of the Sri Lankan people. Here a Buddhist shrine sits nestled amongst paddy fields.*

CONTENTS

TOURIST AREAS

INDEX

For ease of use, the Index has been divided into two sections:

- the first focuses on the Tourist Area Maps and related text and photographs.
- the second deals with the Main Map Section only, facilitating the easy location of cities, towns and villages.

MAIN MAP SECTION

National Route Planner

Legend and Location

National road Nationalstraße Route nationale	
Main road Hauptstraße Route principale	
Secondary road Nebenstraße Route secondaire	
Track Sandpiste Piste/Sentier	
Distance in kilometres Entfernung in Kilometern Distance en kilomètres	19 15
Railway Eisenbahn Chemin de fer	
Provincial boundary Provinzgrenze Frontière provinciale	
District boundary Bezirksgrenze Frontière de district	
Route number Routennummer Numéro de route	A1 42
Airport Flughafen Aéroport	INT Other
City Großstadt Ville	COLOMBO
Major Town Kreisstadt Ville importante	Moratuwa
Town Stadt Ville secondaire	Panadura
Large village Größere Ortschaft Grand village	Gampaha
Village Dorf Village	Seeduwa
Viewpoint Aussichtspunkt Point de vue	Ella Gap
Place of interest Sehenswürdigkeit Endroit à visiter	Clock Tower
Water feature Gewässer Eau	River, Dam
Waterfall Wasserfall Chute d'eau	Elgin
Reef Riff Récif	Coral Gardens
Province name Provinzname Nom de la province	Western Province
District name Bezirksname Nom du District	Matara District
Ruin Ruine Ruines	Pubbarama
Lighthouse Leuchtturm Phare	
Cave Höhle Grotte	Belilena
Hindu Temple Hindutempel Temple Hindou	Hindu Kovil
Buddhist Temple Buddhistentempel Temple Bouddhiste	Nakha Vihara
Monastery Kloster Monastère	Malvatta Monastery
Fort Burg Château	Dutch Fort
Peak in metres Höhe in Metern Altitude (en mètres)	Haycock 661 m
Museum Museum Museu	Dutch Period Museum
Embassy Botschaft Ambassade	Spain
Bank Bank Banque	Bank of Ceylon HQ
Church Kirche Église	St Peter's
Mosque Moschee Mosquée	Grand Mosque
Nature reserve and park Naturschutzgebiet und Park Réserve naturelle et parc	Horton Plains National Park
Beach Strand Plage	
Ferry route Fährverbindung Ferry/bac	F
Golf course Golfplatz Terrain de golf	Nuwawra Eliya Golf Club
Hot spring Heiße Quelle Fontaine chaud	Hot Springs
Spring Quelle Fontaine	Spring
Main road Hauptstraße Route principale	Peradeniya
Road Straße Route	Raja Veediya
Wall Mauer Remparts	
Building of interest Interessantes Bauwerke Edifice intéressant	World Trade Centre
Parking area Parkplatz Parking	P
Restaurant Restaurant Restaurant	Restaurant
Hotel (selected) Hotel (Auswahl) Hôtel (sélectionné)	CARLTON
Hospital Krankenhaus Hôpital	General Hospital
Post office Postamt Bureau de poste	
Information centre Auskunftsbüro Centre d'information	i
Bus terminus Busbahnhof Terminus d'autobus	Inter City Buses
Built-up area Wohngebiet Agglomération	
Library Bibliothek Bibliothèque	
Shopping Centre Einkaufszentrum Centre commercial	S
Gate Tor Porte	Old Gate
University Universität Université	University of Kelaniya
College College College	Trinity College
Safe bathing beach Badestrand Baignade autorisée	
Water sport Wassersport Sports nautiques	W
Snorkelling Schnorcheln Plongée avec tuba	

Tourist Area Planner

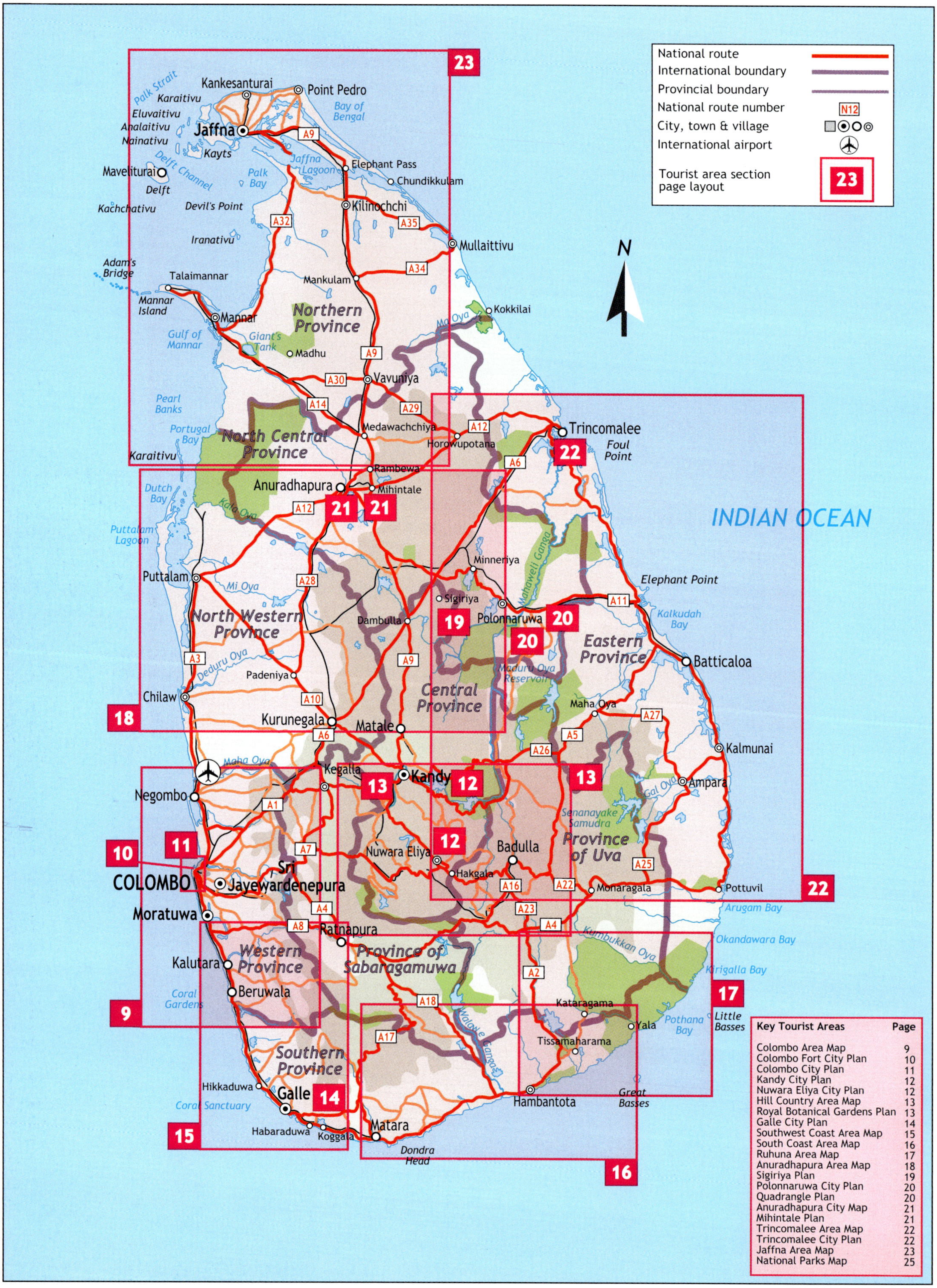

Key Tourist Areas

Key Tourist Areas	Page
Colombo Area Map	9
Colombo Fort City Plan	10
Colombo City Plan	11
Kandy City Plan	12
Nuwara Eliya City Plan	12
Hill Country Area Map	13
Royal Botanical Gardens Plan	13
Galle City Plan	14
Southwest Coast Area Map	15
South Coast Area Map	16
Ruhuna Area Map	17
Anuradhapura Area Map	18
Sigiriya Plan	19
Polonnaruwa City Plan	20
Quadrangle Plan	20
Anuradhapura City Map	21
Mihintale Plan	21
Trincomalee Area Map	22
Trincomalee City Plan	22
Jaffna Area Map	23
National Parks Map	25

Distance and Climate Charts

Climate Charts

These charts show the average temperature and rainfall for the main towns or areas of Sri Lanka.

COLOMBO	J	F	M	A	M	J	J	A	S	O	N	D
AVERAGE TEMP. °F	79	80	81	82	83	81	81	81	81	80	79	79
AVERAGE TEMP. °C	26	27	27	28	29	27	27	27	27	27	26	26
RAINFALL in	3.5	2.7	5.8	9.1	14.6	8.8	5.3	4.3	6.3	13.7	12.4	5.8
RAINFALL mm	89	69	147	231	371	224	135	109	160	348	315	147
Days of Rainfall	7	6	8	14	19	18	12	11	13	19	16	10

TRINCOMALEE	J	F	M	A	M	J	J	A	S	O	N	D
AVERAGE TEMP. °F	78	79	81	84	86	86	85	85	85	82	80	78
AVERAGE TEMP. °C	26	26	27	29	30	30	30	30	30	28	27	26
RAINFALL in	6.8	2.6	1.9	2.3	2.7	1.1	2.0	4.2	4.2	8.7	14.1	14.3
RAINFALL mm	173	66	48	58	69	28	51	107	107	221	358	363
Days of Rainfall	10	4	4	5	5	2	3	6	6	13	17	16

NUWARA ELIYA	J	F	M	A	M	J	J	A	S	O	N	D
AVERAGE TEMP. °F	57	57	58	60	62	61	60	61	60	60	60	58
AVERAGE TEMP. °C	14	14	15	16	17	16	16	16	16	16	16	15
RAINFALL in	6.7	1.7	4.3	4.7	6.9	10.9	11.8	7.7	8.9	10.6	9.5	8.0
RAINFALL mm	170	43	109	119	175	277	300	196	226	269	241	203
Days of Rainfall	13	6	11	15	18	25	25	22	20	22	22	17

Above: *Leopards are one of the most secretive and rare animals on Sri Lanka, but these cubs play happily in the open.*

Distance Chart

In order to calculate the distance between two of the country's major centres, locate the name of the first town or city on the vertical or horizontal column on the chart (see below), then locate the name of the other on the second column and read off the number where the vertical and horizontal lines intersect.

APPROXIMATE DISTANCES IN KILOMETRES & MILES	AMPARA	ANURADHAPURA	BADULLA	BATTICALOA	COLOMBO	GALLE	HAMBANTOTA	JAFFNA	KALUTARA	KANDY	KANKESANTURAI	KEGALLA	KURUNEGALA	MANNAR	MATALE	MATARE	NUWARA ELIYA	PANADURA	POLONNARUWA	PUTTALAM	RATNAPURA	TALAIMANNAR	TRINCOMALEE	VAVUNIYA	WELLAWAYA
AMPARA		269	172	70	350	332	209	469	335	185	483	224	227	381	206	288	222	318	185	311	245	408	206	308	128
ANURADHAPURA	167		272	196	206	322	364	195	249	138	212	153	121	111	113	367	216	233	101	74	240	138	106	53	296
BADULLA	43	169		167	230	256	134	454	206	134	472	159	175	370	159	211	56	198	233	262	129	398	277	312	53
BATTICALOA	43	122	104		303	381	261	378	346	187	396	225	217	295	212	336	224	328	95	270	296	322	138	237	179
COLOMBO	217	128	143	188		116	238	396	43	116	414	77	93	312	142	160	180	27	216	142	101	340	257	254	222
GALLE	206	200	159	237	72		124	512	72	232	529	192	209	428	257	45	290	89	332	248	150	455	373	370	203
HAMBANTOTA	130	226	83	162	148	77		546	193	245	563	227	243	462	270	77	167	211	323	330	124	489	367	404	80
JAFFNA	291	121	282	235	246	318	339		439	320	18	335	303	219	295	557	398	323	283	269	422	246	238	142	484
KALUTARA	206	155	128	215	27	45	120	273		159	457	121	137	356	185	116	192	16	259	175	77	283	301	298	198
KANDY	115	86	83	116	72	144	152	199	99		338	39	42	237	26	277	77	143	140	129	142	264	182	179	164
KANKESANTURAI	300	132	293	246	257	329	350	11	284	210		352	320	237	312	575	415	441	301	286	439	264	256	159	502
KEGALLA	139	95	99	140	48	119	141	208	75	24	219		32	251	64	238	103	105	154	119	103	278	196	193	198
KURUNEGALA	141	75	109	135	58	130	151	188	85	26	199	20		219	68	254	119	121	122	87	119	246	164	161	206
MANNAR	237	69	230	183	194	266	287	136	221	147	147	156	136		211	473	314	340	200	185	338	27	174	77	402
MATALE	128	70	99	132	88	160	168	183	115	16	194	40	42	131		303	103	169	144	154	168	238	156	153	192
MATARE	179	228	131	209	100	28	48	346	72	172	357	148	158	294	188		245	132	377	293	169	501	418	415	158
NUWARA ELIYA	138	134	35	139	112	180	104	247	119	48	258	64	74	195	64	152		182	217	206	148	341	259	256	87
PANADURA	198	145	123	204	17	55	131	201	10	89	274	65	75	211	105	82	113		243	159	69	367	285	282	190
POLONNARUWA	115	63	145	59	134	206	201	176	161	87	187	96	76	124	89	89	135	151		175	241	227	129	142	243
PUTTALAM	193	46	163	168	88	154	205	167	109	80	178	74	54	115	96	182	128	99	109		206	212	180	127	295
RATNAPURA	152	149	80	184	68	93	77	262	48	88	273	64	74	210	104	105	92	43	150	128		365	283	280	121
TALAIMANNAR	253	86	247	200	211	283	304	153	176	164	164	173	153	17	148	311	212	228	141	132	227		201	105	430
TRINCOMALEE	128	66	172	86	160	232	228	148	187	113	159	122	102	108	97	260	161	177	80	112	176	125		97	286
VAVUNIYA	191	33	194	147	158	230	251	88	185	111	99	120	100	48	95	257	159	175	88	79	174	65	60		344
WELLAWAYA	80	184	33	111	138	126	50	301	223	102	312	123	126	250	119	98	54	118	151	183	75	267	178	214	

KILOMETRES

MILES

Colombo Area

Colombo's urban sprawl has pushed the city limits northwards and southwards. These residential suburbs and resort areas have the beaches closest to the city centre, and as a result were the first to be developed for beach tourism. Negombo has the virtue of being the closest beach resort to Katunayake International Airport while Mount Lavinia, south of the capital, was a favourite with the British colonial classes. Fishing has provided many generations of villagers with a living. Today, tourist hotels and restaurants offer a ready market for the fish, prawns and lobsters of the lagoons and offshore waters. The region boasts more than a dozen luxury resort hotels.

Travel Tips

The Sri Lanka Tourist Board, 80 Galle Road, Colombo 3, tel: (011) 243 7059, fax: (011) 243 7953, www.srilankatourism.org is the place to stock up on island information.

Negombo makes an ideal first-night stop after a tiring flight or last evening finale to a touring holiday, since it is so convenient for the international airport.

Health Hazards

Before travelling to Sri Lanka consult with your doctor about a health plan that updates all necessary vaccinations for your trip. If neccesary, anti Malarial treatment may need to be started early and some inoculations must be administered in several doses over a number of weeks prior to your departure.

Main Attractions

Negombo, 37km (23 miles) north of Colombo city centre, offers picturesque narrow streets and colourful stucco. The resort is nicknamed 'Little Rome' because of its numerous Catholic churches – a survival from the period of Dutch rule – of which St Mary's Church with its painted ceiling is the most interesting. Negombo surrounds a lagoon that is rich in fish, prawns and lobster, ingredients that enhance the menus of many of the island's best restaurants. A ruined Dutch fort dating from 1678 commands the entrance to the lagoon. Next to the walls is a Dutch cemetery.

Mount Lavinia, 11km (6 miles) south of Colombo, was Sri Lanka's first beach resort when British Governor Sir Thomas Maitland built an official residence here in around 1805-6. He named the house after his then mistress, Lavinia. It was rebuilt in the 1820s by one of his successors, Edward Barnes, before it became a government rest home, and in 1895 was transformed into the Mount Lavinia Hotel. Modern extensions now surround the historical core.

Kalutara is a bustling village at the mouth of the Kalu Ganga, 45km (27 miles) south of Colombo. Famed for its coconuts – both fruit and fibre products – you can see baskets being woven at the Basket Centre in the middle of the village. This is also a good place to buy genuine Sri Lankan handmade coconut fibre souvenirs including the aforesaid baskets, floor and table mats, and coasters.

On the banks of the **Kalu Ganga**, next to the road bridge, stands the **Gangatilaka Vihara**, a large and hollow dagoba (Buddhist shrine) with an unusual painted interior, beside which stands a Sacred Bo Tree.

Top: *Negombo's many Catholic churches are a legacy of the Portuguese colonial era.*
Above: *The traditional, hand-built, wooden catamaran has served Sri Lankan fisherman well for many generations.*

Colombo Area
Gampaha District
Colombo District
Kalutara District
Kegalla District
Western Province
Province of Sabaragamuwa
COLOMBO
Sri Jayewardenepura
Dehiwala-Mount Lavinia
Negombo
Dutch Fort
St Mary
Negombo Lagoon
Bolawatta
Kochchikade
Katana
Godigomuwa
Kotadeniyawa
Dunagaha
Diwulapitiya
Mirigama
Ambepussa
Warakapola
Nelundeniya
Galigomuwa
Dedigama
Kota Vihara
Archaeological Museum
Pindeniya
Galapitamada
Salgala
Pallewela
Minuwangoda
Veyangoda
Pasyala
Nittambuwa
Attanagalla
Urapola
Kurana
Katunayake
Seeduwa
Pamunugama
Kotugoda
Udugampola
Henarathgoda Botanical Gardens
Gampaha
Yakkala
Varana
Ja-Ela
Ganemulla
Miriswatta
Gonagalderiya
Anguruwella
Ruwanwella
Kandana
Ragama
Weliweriya
Henegama
Radawana
Kirindiwela
Weke
Karawanella
Yatiyantota
Welisara
Kadawata
Hendala
Dalugama
Raja Maha Vihara
Pugoda
Dehiowita
Royal Colombo Yacht Club
Peliyagoda
Kelaniya
Malwana
Dompe
Kosgama
Avissawella
Kotikawatta
Kaduwela
Kelani Ganga
Puwakpitiya
Palace, Berendi Kovil
Royal Colombo Golf Club
Hanwella
Getahetta
Kalatuwawa Reservoir
Waga
Maharagama
Eheliyagoda
Kottawa
Homagama
Labugama Reservoir
Parakaduwa
Kesbewa
Kahutuduwa
Handapangoda
Bolgoda Lake
Moratuwa
Ceylon Motor Yacht Club
Gonapola
Egoda Uyana
Widiyagoda
Kalupahana
Ingiriya
Idangoda
Nambapana
Kiriella
Panadura
Horana
Kalu Ganga
Alubomulla
Bandaragama
Tuttiripitiya
Gonaduwa
Egaloya
Bulathsinhala
Wadduwa
Kehellenawa
Ayagama
Waskaduwa
Gangatilaka Vihara
Tebuwana
Mahagama
Kalutara
Neboda
Katukurunda
Nagoda
Pimbura
Dodangoda
Agalawatta
Bellana
Lathpandura
Paiyagala
Eladuwa
Matugama
Badureliya
Maggona
Kechchimalai Mosque
Horawala
Beruwala
Kirantidiya
Coral Gardens
Welipenna
Moragala
N
3000m+
2000-3000m
1000-2000m
500-1000m
200-500m
100-200m
0-100m
Scale 1: 400 000
0 5 10 km
0 2.5 5 miles

Colombo City

Sri Lanka's bustling capital is located on the country's west coast. It has by far the biggest urban population on the island (estimates vary between 800,000 and one million) and is the island's window on the world. This fine natural harbour on the River Kelani was a magnet for successive traders and conquerors – first Arab merchants, then Portuguese, Dutch and British imperialists – but today's city is a sometimes jarring mixture of old and new, with a cluster of high-rise office blocks and hotels overshadowing low-rise red-tiled colonial-era buildings, venerated Buddhist viharas, Hindu temples, Muslim mosques and sprawling street markets, all of which buzz with life during daylight hours when 400,000 commuting workers go about their business. It's a great place to explore on foot.

Main Attractions

The central area of the city, **Fort**, settled by the Portuguese, is the financial and commercial heart of the city. The 19th-century **Clock Tower** at the corner of Janadhipathi Mawatha and Chatham Street was once a lighthouse but is now a city landmark.

Visit **Cargill's Department Store** on York Street, which is little changed since it was built by the Victorians to supply their colonial civil servants and plantation owners.

Neighbouring **Pettah** – east of Fort across a narrow canal – is the market district, an aromatic, bustling and totally beguiling area where you can buy almost anything from sapphires to spices. The **Gold Souk** is one of the world's best in terms of quality to price, and also because bespoke pieces can be made to order in only a few days.

Colombo's museums are a must in understanding the complex history of the nation. The **National Museum** has the most comprehensive collection of artefacts and artwork that spans several centuries and runs the whole gamut of cultures. The **Dutch Period Museum** offers a glimpse of life under Dutch rule and is housed in a mansion built for the head of the Dutch East India Company. Nearby **Wolvendaal Church** (1749) contains the tombs of several Dutch governors.

Above: *Cargill's store has changed little since the days of the British Empire.*

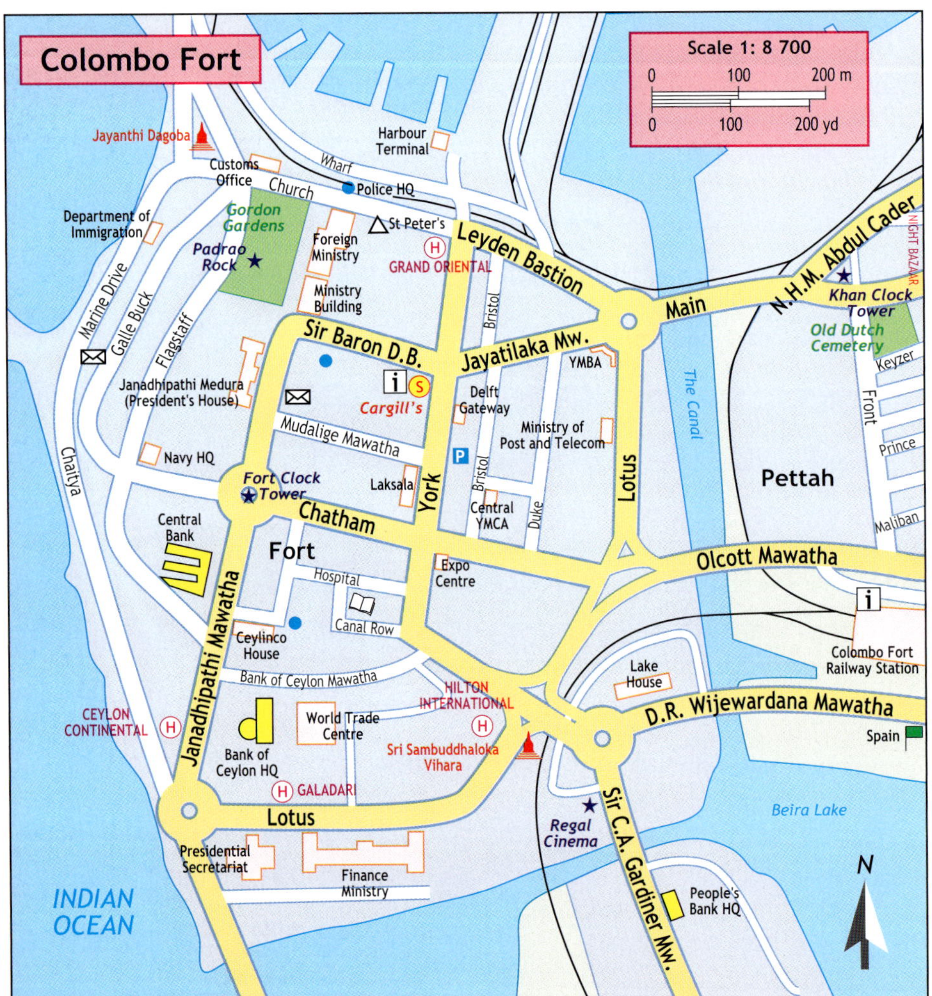

Accommodation

Luxury

Galadari Hotel, 64 Lotus Road, Echelon Square, tel: (011) 254 4544, fax: (011) 244 9875, www.lanka.net/galadari The best value five-star in town, with its own nightclub and large-screen cinema.

Ceylon Continental Hotel, 48 Janadhipathi Mawatha, Colombo 1, tel: (011) 242 1221, fax: (011) 244 7326, www.colombocontinental.com Comfortable, recently renovated international chain hotel with large pool and fine sea views from its high-rise rooms.

Mid-range

Hotel Renuka, 328 Galle Road, Colombo 3, tel: (011) 257 3598, fax: (011) 257 4137. Excellent value, medium-sized hotel with air-conditioned rooms, pool and restaurant.

Budget

Sea View Hotel, 15 Sea View Avenue, Colombo 3, tel/fax: (011) 257 3570. Reliable, reasonably priced and central, but no view of the sea!

Colombo City
Queen Elizabeth Quay
Bandaranaike Quay
Buddhist Mission Bureau
Harbour Terminal
Jayanthi Dagoba
Customs Office
Church
Dept of Immigration
Ministry Building
St Peter's
Janadhipathi Medura (President's House)
Fort Clock Tower
YMBA
Delft Gateway
Cargill's
Laksala
Chatham
Ceylinco House
Expo Centre
Fort
World Trade Centre
Bank of Ceylon HQ
Presidential Secretariat
Finance Ministry
Lake House
Sri Sambuddhaloka Vihara
Regal Cinema
Spain
Bandaranaike Statue
Galle Face Green
Rifle Green
Fort Tennis Club
TRANS ASIA
Beira Lake
Slave Island
Glennie
Malay
NIPPON
TAJ SAMUDRA
Slave Island Railway Station
Christ Church
Church
KOLUU'S REST
HOLIDAY INN
Gem Corp.
GALLE FACE
Indian High Commission
USA Consulate
Sri Bodhiraja Vidyalaya
St Andrew's Scot's Kirk
Amusement Park
Sima Malaka Meditation Centre
Perahera Mw.
Hudson
Alwis Pl.
Dharamakirthiyamaraya
Prime Minister's Office
CRESCAT
Muhandiram's
Great Britain
USA
St Michael
St Michael's
Liberty Cinema
Kollupitiya Railway Station
Amaravadai
Bulgaria
Belgium
SEA VIEW
RENUKA
Ayurvedic
Kollupitiya Ln.
Deanston Pl.
5th Lane
Togo
Durdens Private Hospital
Mumtaz Mahal
Charles Dr.
Alfred Pl.
Baptist Church
Switzerland
Walukarama Temple
27th Lane
Flower Tce
Unity Pl.
Colonel T.G. Jayawardana Mw.
INDIAN OCEAN
Galle Face Drive
Galle Face Centre
Baladaksah Mw.
Janadhipathi Mw.
Chaitya
Galle
R.A. de Mel Mw.
Sir Chittampalam A. Gardiner Mw.
Sir James Peiris Mw.
Union Place
Navaloka
Ratnam's Private Hospital
Vauxhall
Sri Lanka Fraud Bureau
Turkey
Staple
Dawson
YWCA
Empire Cinema
Baybroke
Muttah
Park
Sri Jinarathana
Liberia
Gangaramaya Bhikku
W.A.D. Ramanayaka Mw.
Hyde Park Corner
Hyde Park
Sweden
The Commons
Korea
Sir Marcus Fernando
Sir Ernest de Silva Mw.
Ananda Kumaraswamy Mw.
Mayor's Residence
Srawasthie
American Centre
Dharmapala Mw.
Viharamahadevi Statue
Viharamahadevi Park
War Memorial
Public Library
National Art Gallery
John de Silva Memorial Theatre
Archaeological Dept
National Museum
Town Hall
Davatagaha Mosque
Baptist Church
Albert Crescent
Australia
Russian Cultural Dept
St Bridget's Montisoori
Cambridge Place
Guildford Crescent
Lionel Wendt Theatre & Art Gallery
Rajakeeya Mw.
Sri Lanka Library Services
National Archives
Ministry of Foreign Affairs
Cinnamon Gardens
Ministry of Textile Industry
Sri Lanka Broadcasting Corp.
Independence Ave
Maitland Place
Maitland Crescent
Ministry of Public Administration
Bandaranaike Memorial International Conference Hall & Museum
Bauddhaloka Mw.
Aukana Buddha Replica
Kelaniya Rajamaha Vihara
Vidyalaya Mw.
China
Vidya Mandiraya
Wijerama Mw.
Canada
Philippines
Japan
Gregory's
Finland
University of Kelaniya
German Cultural Institute
Horton Place
Korea
Libya
Slovakia
C.W.W. Kannangara Mw.
Barnes Place
Thailand
Iraq
MacCarthy
Russia
France
Rosmead Place
Netherlands
Norway
Ward Place
Police Hospital
Wijerama Mw.
Yasodara Maha Vidyalaya
Accident Care
Norris Canal
Colombo General
Kynsey
Francis
E.W. Perera Mw.
Eye Hospital
Foster
De Saram Place
Dutch Reformed
Deans
Canal
Vipulasena Mw.
Vinayalankara Mw.
Mahabodhi Vidyalaya
Viharamahadevi Balika Vidyalaya
A. Ratnayake Mw.
Fire Brigade
T.B. Jayah Mw.
Maradana
New Olympic Cinema
Maradana Mosque
Symmonds
P. Sirisena Mw.
J.E. Gunasekara Ave
Kularatna Mw.
Temple
Gotami Balika Maha Vidyalaya
Ananda Vidyalaya
Ananda Play Ground
Ananda Mw.
Ananda Balika Vidyalaya
Maligakanda
Mallikananda Maha Vidyalaya
Dharmadutasrama Vidyalaya
Sri Vajiragnana Mw.
Maradana Railway Station
Orasipasha
Elvinstone Theatre
Sarasavipaya
Tower Hall Theatre
Jayantha Weerasekara Mw.
Abhayasingh660aramaya
Ruby Cinema
Government Hospital
Sri Sangaraja Madya Maha Vidyalaya
Panchikawatta
Al-Hadiiyar Maha Vidyalaya
Hulftsdorf
Kovil
Olcott Mw.
Postal Dept Transport Office
Colombo Fort Railway Station
D.R. Wijewardana Mw.
E.W. Bastian Mw.
Olcott Mw.
Manning Market
Mihindu Mw.
Bus to Airport
CTB Central
St Sebastian Hill
All Saints
St Sebastian
Dias Pl.
Saunders Pl.
Bodhiraja
4th Cross
3rd Cross
2nd Cross
Maliban
Dutch Period Museum
Keyzer
Front
Pettah
Lotus
Khan Clock Tower
Night Bazaar
Main
Market
Old Town Hall & Museum
Bankhall
N.H.M. Abdul Cader
Fish Market
Colombo Central
Central
Ganeshan Temple
Hindu Kathiresan Kovil
Old Kathiresan Kovil
Sea
St Kathiresan
St Anthony Mw.
R. Saravanamuttu Mw.
Wolvendaal
Clock Tower
Gintupitiya
Murugan Theatre
Ratnam
Vivakananda Hill
St Mary's
New Chetty
Vivekanada Maha Vidyalaya
Jampettah
Sangamitta Mw.
Green Ln.
Sellamahal Cinema
Kingsley Theatre
Naha Vidyala Mw.
Husainia St
Grand Mosque
New Moor
Old Moor
Dam
M.J.M. Lafeer Mw.
Srimath Bandaranaike Mw.
Belmont
Meeraniya
Princes Gate
Crown Cinema
Pradeepa Mw.
New Town
Sri Sumanatissa Mw.
Grandpass
Sulaiman
Capitol Cinema
Jetawana
Jetawanaramaya Temple
Isipathanaramaya
Jayasekararama Viharaya
Kettarama Play Ground
Srimath Baron Jayathilaka Vidyalaya
M.J. Masjid
Lukmanjee Sq.
Dr Babapulle Pl.
Jayanthi Vidyalaya
Awwal Zaviya
Swarna Chaitya
Temple
Scale 1: 18 000
0
250
500 m
0
250
500 yd
N

Kandy and the Hill Country

The heart of Sri Lanka offers a wonderful contrast to the coastal plains; with cool, lush mountain scenery it is a very different aspect of Sri Lanka, one that those visitors who restrict their stay to the coastal resorts never see. This region was the traditional base for the Kings of Sri Lanka who ruled from a capital at Kandy. Later colonial power brokers preferred to take advantage of the climate for the production of tea and other plantation crops, or as an escape from the stifling heat of their offices in Colombo. Today's visitors will discover a range of attractions from working plantations, spectacular gardens, exquisite temples and the promise of riches in gems and precious stones.

Accommodation

Nuwara Eliya

Ceylon Tea Trails, Dickoya, tel: (052) 230 3888, fax: (052) 230 3999, www.teatrails.com A small collection of luxurious bungalows built for tea plantation managers and set in the heart of hill country.

St Andrew's Hotel, 10 St Andrew's Drive, Nuwara Eliya, tel: (052) 222 2445, fax: (052) 222 3153. Comfortable, recently modernized accommodation in a colonial-style hotel – originally the 19th-century clubhouse of the region's Scottish planters. Four-poster beds, attractive garden.

Grand Hotel, Grand Hotel Road, Nuwara Eliya, tel: (052) 222 2881, fax: (052) 222 2264, www.tangerinehotels.com Nuwara Eliya's poshest hotel, next to the golf course. Billiard room, bars; reeks of the jolly old British Empire.

The Tea Factory, Kandapola, Nuwara Eliya, tel: (052) 222 3600, fax: (052) 222 2026, www.aitkenspencehotels.com Hotel of character located in the restored buildings of a former tea plantation. Good value.

Ratnapura

Ratnaloka Tour Inn, Kosgala, Kahangama, Ratnapura, tel: (045) 222 2455, fax: (045) 222 2350. Adequate, reasonable value for money; the only place to stay in Ratnapura!

Above: *Adam's Peak is a sacred spot revered by all the religious communities of Sri Lanka.*

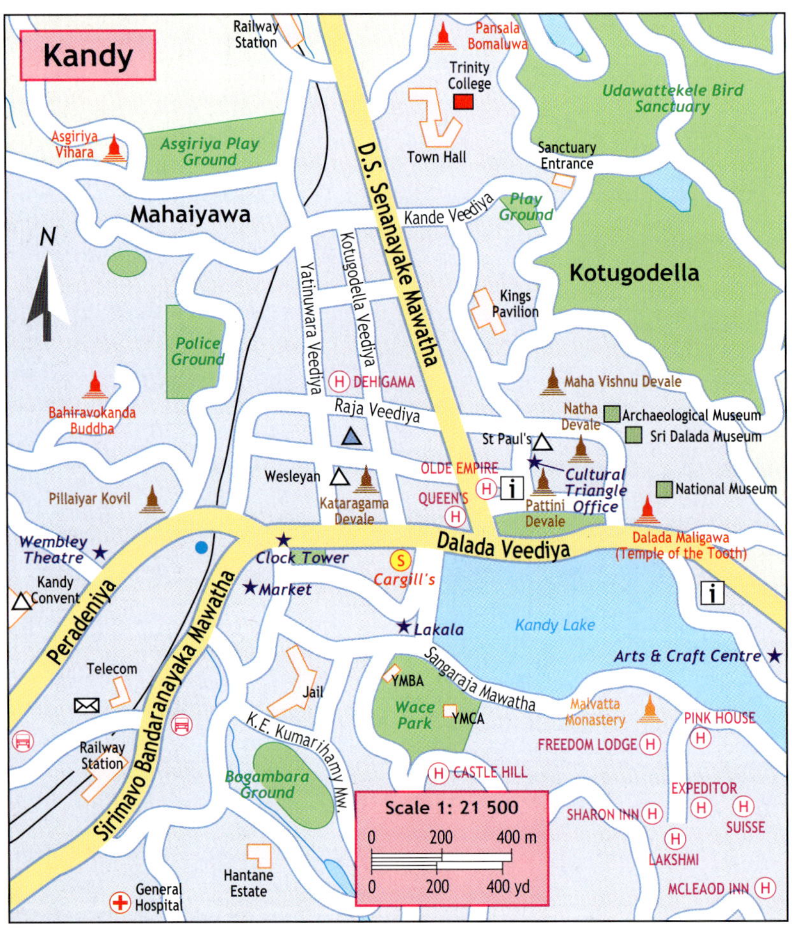

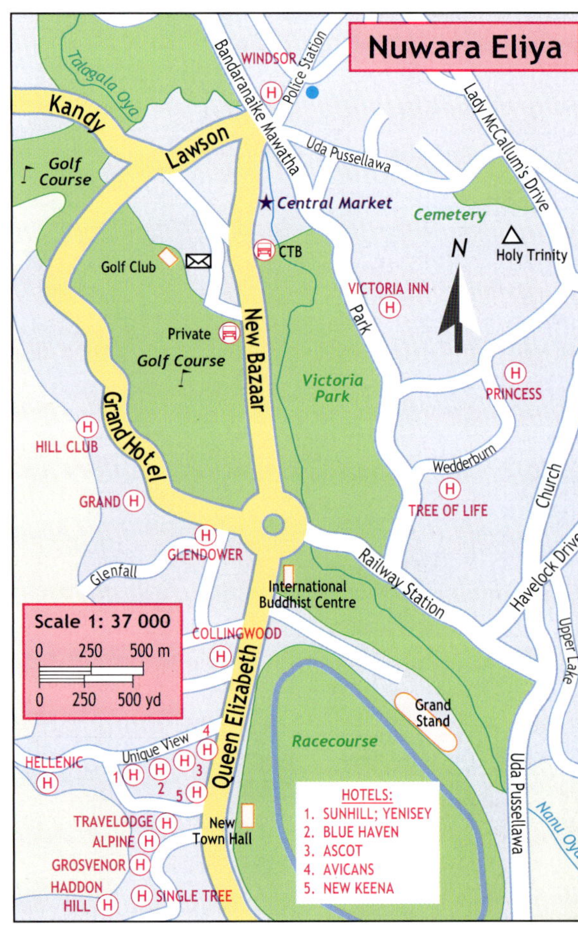

Main Attractions

For the City of Kandy *see* page 51. Close by to the west, the **Pinnewala Elephant Orphanage** is one of the world's most famed wildlife attractions, where the young elephants are cared for and educated. **Nuwara Eliya** to the southwest is the heart of tea country, with architecture reminiscent of colonial England and a decidedly temperate climate. The southern slopes of the region are bounded by two important protected landscapes, **Horton Plains National Park** with its high-land miniature forests and World's End sheer drop-off, and **Peak Wilderness Sanctuary**, land surrounding **Adam's Peak** (Sri Pada), the 2243m (7359ft) mountain considered a holy site by all Sri Lankan religions for a foot-print said to be that of Adam, Shiva or St Thomas, depending on belief. On the southwestern boundary of Hill Country, visit the small town of **Ratnapura**, famed for its gems and minerals.

Useful Contacts

Sri Lanka Wildlife Conservation Society (www.slwcs.org) is a US-based charitable organization that aims to protect native fauna through sustainable con-servation. They have information on a wide diversity of eco-programmes on the island. The society can also organize short volunteer programmes for tourists interested in working on conservation on the island.

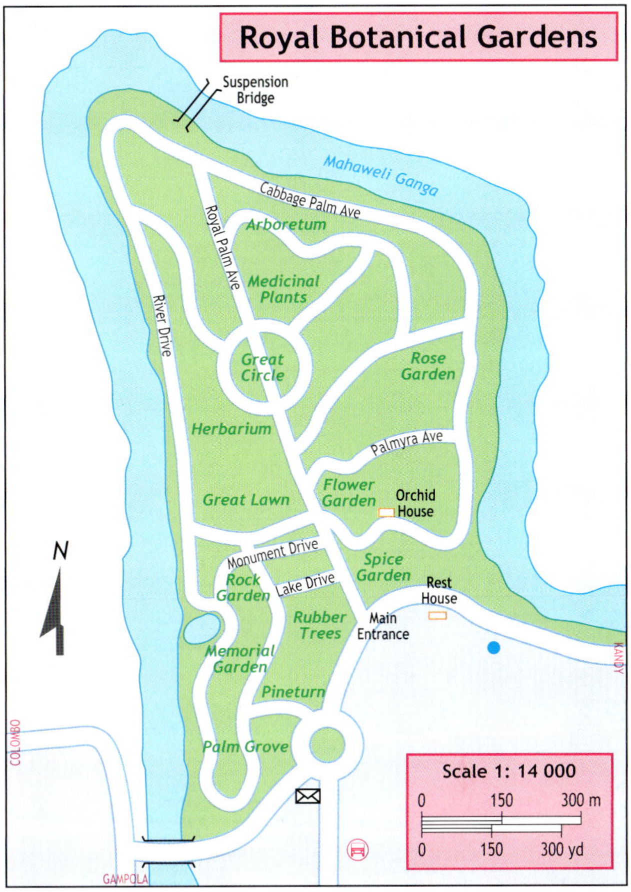

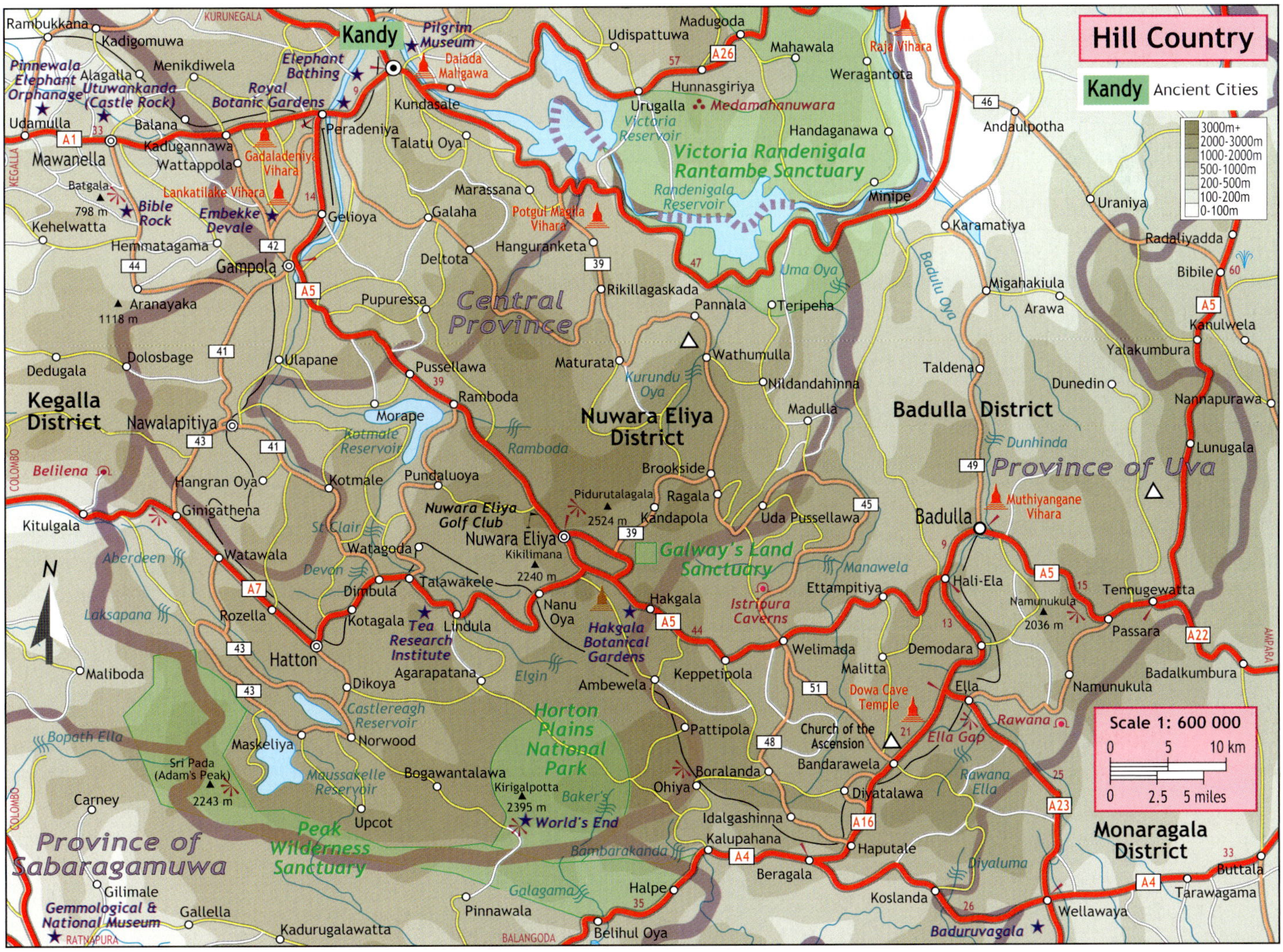

Galle and the Southwest

The coast south of Colombo is Sri Lanka's most popular holiday resort area, with fine beaches of golden sand lined with coconut palms, where traditional outrigger canoes are still hauled up in front of gleaming new holiday hotels. Yet there are still miles of uncrowded coastline to explore, where tourism has had little impact. The beaches are the biggest attraction of this part of the island, but the region has more to offer than lounging beneath the palms. Offshore, there are some excellent dive sites; Galle, the largest town in the region, is full of history, while inland it's an easy trip to the lush interior.

Above left: *Lighthouses have been invaluable in protecting shipping around the treacherous reefs lying just offshore, and guiding ships safely into Sri Lanka's harbours.*

Travel Tips

Many travel agencies offer a range of tours of the ancient cities of **Anuradhapura**, **Polonnaruwa** and **Sigiriya**, **Kandy** and the hill country, and **Ruhuna National Park** in the southeast. All mid-range and luxury hotels have tour desks offering a full range of excursions. Most resort hotels on the southwest coast can arrange scuba diving trips and deep-sea fishing.

Regular rail services between Colombo, Galle and Matara offer a different way to enjoy Sri Lanka and meet the local people.

Main Attractions

Galle's centuries-old ramparts and bastions constitute one of the best-preserved colonial-era cities in Southeast Asia and have been declared a World Heritage site. Inside are numerous buildings dating from the Dutch era, including the **Old Dutch Government House** (now the offices of a shipping company), the **Governor's House** (now a hotel), and the **Groote Kerk** (Great Church), built in 1755 and still in use by worshippers.

South of Galle town you can watch Sri Lanka's famed stilt fishermen ply their trade just offshore at Weligama, while 20km inland is another UNESCO World Heritage site, **Sinharaja Biosphere Reserve**, a long 'island' of lowland rainforest regarded as one of the most important and bio-diverse conservation areas in Sri Lanka.

Note that there are further attractions in the Galle District (*see* pages 56-57).

Accommodation

Bentota

Bentota Beach Hotel, National Holiday Resort, tel: (034) 227 5176/7, fax: (034) 228 1603. Four-star hotel with gardens, pool, water sports and view of the sea and Bentota River.

Beruwala

Eden Hotel, Kaluwamodara, tel: (034) 227 6075, fax: (034) 227 6181. Five-star with pool, Jacuzzi, disco, tennis courts, water sports and marina.

Hikkaduwa

Hotel Lanka Supercorals, 390 Galle Road, tel: (091) 227 7387, fax (091) 238 3385, www.hotellankasupercorals.com Deluxe rooms, garden, pool, TV lounge, kids' corner and pizza restaurant.

Galle

Lighthouse Hotel, Dadella, Galle, tel: (091) 222 3744, fax: (091) 222 4021, www.jetwing.net/lighthouse Exclusive luxury hotel with large pool, palm-fringed beach and grounds.

Ahungalla

Triton Hotel, Ahungalla, tel: (091) 226 4041, fax: (091) 226 4046, www.aitkenspencehotels.com Superbly luxurious beach resort on its own beach.

Unawatuna

Unawatuna Beach Resort, Unawatuna, Galle, tel: (091) 438 4545, fax: (091) 223 2247, www.unawatunabeachresort.com Scuba centre, beach, Ayurvedic health club.

Top: *A modern fishing fleet caters to a growing demand for fish.*
Below: *The famous stilt fishermen of Sri Lanka's south coast ply their unique trade.*

The South Coast

East of Galle lie some of Sri Lanka's finest beaches, delightfully unexploited by mainstream tourism but offering enough places to stay to make it an ideal location for a simple, away-from-it-all beach holiday. Spread out along the south coast are small fishing ports, superb white sand beaches, and offshore there are a number of excellent reef and wreck dives, while the region also has some of Sri Lanka's finest wildlife sanctuaries. Sri Lanka's south coast is one of the most attractive parts of the island; Its array of natural wonders is complemented by a fascinating selection of man-made attractions, ranging from Buddhist and Hindu shrines to Dutch colonial fortresses.

Accommodation

Matara

Polhena Reef Garden Hotel, 30 Beach Road, Polhena, tel: (041) 222 2478. Affordable, simple hotel.

Tangalla

Club Dikwella Village, for reservations/information contact Connaissance de Ceyland Ltd., 58 Dudley Senanayake Mawatha, Colombo 8, tel: (011) 268 5601, fax: (011) 268 5555, www.dikwellavillage.com

Talalla Retreat, Talalla South, Gandara, tel: (041) 225 9171, fax: (041) 203 9515, www.talallaretreat.com Well-planned accommodation and a host of wellbeing treatments, including detox, yoga and reflexology.

Hambantota

Hotel Oasis, Sisilasagama, tel: (047) 223 0650, fax: (047) 222 0651. Comfortable tourist hotel with good location.

Tissamaharama

Tissamaharama Rest House, tel: (047) 223 7299, fax: (047) 223 7201. Best place to stay in Tissa; pool, lake view, restaurant.

Uda Walawe National Park

Centauria Tourist Hotel, New Town, Embelipitiya, tel: (047) 223 0104. Basic small guesthouse close to the park entrance

Ruhuna National Park

Yala Village Hotel PO Box 1, Kirinda, Tissamaharama, Tel: (047) 223 9450, fax: (047) 223 9450, www.yalavillage.com A very relaxing property set in ten acres. Chalets set at the forest edge with access to lagoon and marine environments.

Above: *The Hindu Kataragama Kavadi is one of Sri Lanka's many colourful religious festivals.*
Opposite: *Spotted deer in Uda Walawe National Park.*

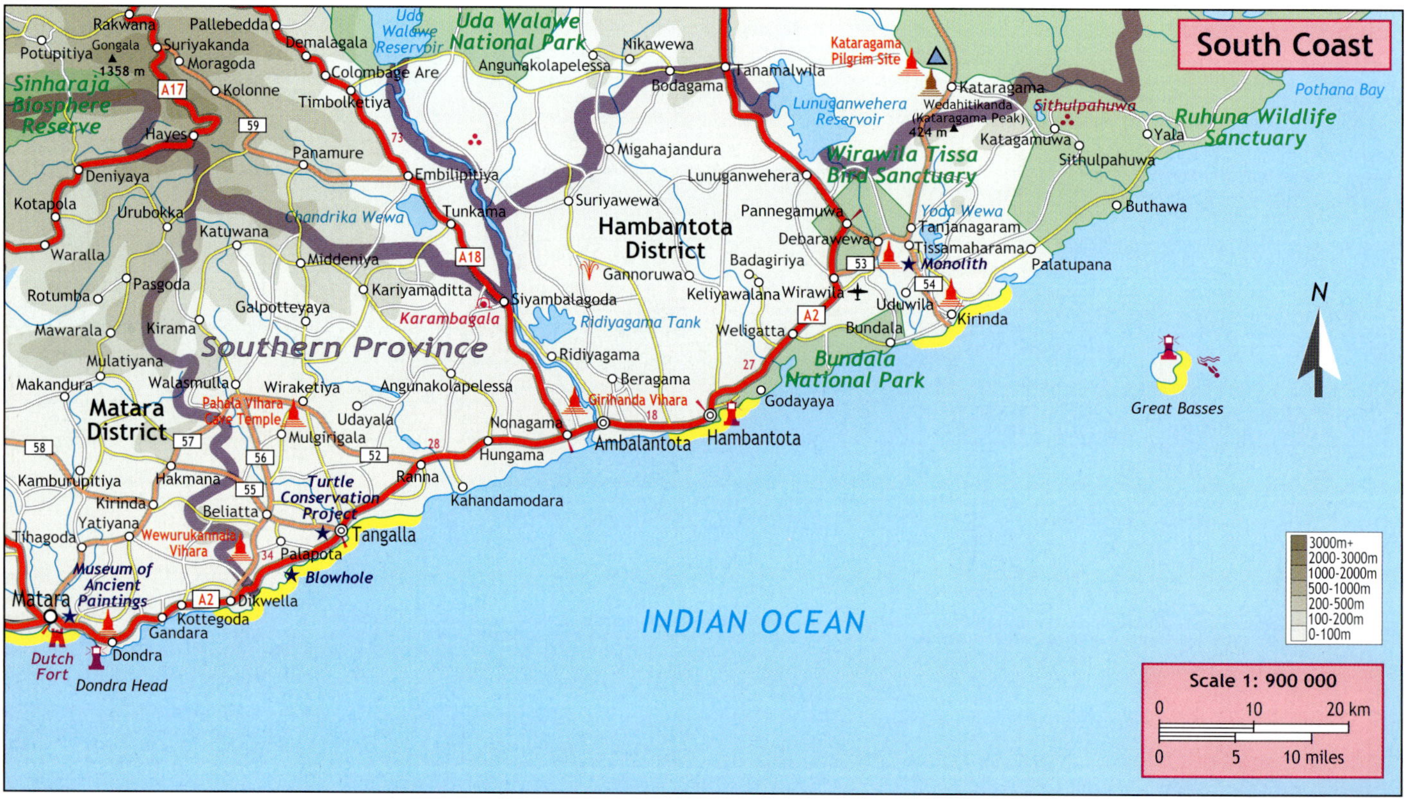

Main Attractions

Matara is the main town along the coast but its colonial treasures are covered in greater detail on page 58. The region is bounded in the east by the district of Hambantota (*see* page 60), a low-key relaxed fishing town-cum-resort. However, most visitors make their way to the south coast to visit one or more of the national parks, the best being the huge **Yala** (Ruhuna) **National Park** (*see* page 62) with its herds of wild elephants; **Bundala National Park** (*see* page 60) is well-known for its birdlife and crocodile population; the **Wirawila Tissa Bird Sanctuary**; and the **Uda Walawe National Park** (*see* page 24). All of these lie in the sparsely populated western fringes.

Tissamaharama (*see* page 60) north-east of Hambantota, makes a convenient jumping-off point for Ruhuna National Park, to the east, and the **Kataragama temple complex**, Sri Lanka's second most sacred place of pilgrimage. Sri Lankan Muslims, Buddhists and Hindus visit en masse in July and August, during the season of pilgrimages and festivals.

Anuradhapura and the Northwest

Compared with the lush greenery of the tea-growing hill country around Kandy, the rolling, open country of Sri Lanka's northwest (also known as the dry zone or 'Cultural Triangle') is arid, coloured in shades of dusty brown earth and golden ripening rice fields. The region contains some of Sri Lanka's most awe-inspiring sights, including temples and fortresses crowning steep rock pinnacles like Sigiriya that rise above the dusty plains, and the ruins of lost ancient cities like Anuradhapura and Polonnaruwa. Huge rock-cut Buddha images, dagobas and cave temples testify to a very ancient Buddhist tradition.

Main Attractions

According to the *Mahavansa*, the epic genealogy of the Sri Lankan kings, Anuradhapura was founded in 457BC by the powerful **King Pandukabaya**. The city was Sri Lanka's capital for over a thousand years and has close ties with the birth and development of Buddhism on the island.

Many of the secular palace buildings were originally made of wood and have not survived; the brick and stone religious treasures, however, leave a lasting impression. At the heart of the complex is **Sri Maha Bodhi** (Sacred Bo Tree), said to be the very tree brought to Sri Lanka by Buddhist Indian Emperor Ashok in the 3rd century BC.

Thuparama Dagoba is the oldest Buddhist reliquary (vatadage) in Sri Lanka (originally 3rd century BC) and contains the collarbone of the Buddha. Looming over the entire site, the **Jetavanarama Dagoba** is almost 122m (400ft) tall with a base diameter of more than 113m (370ft), making it the largest Buddhist building in southern Asia. The neighbouring **Jetavanarama Museum** houses finds from the site. The range of objects on display shows that Anuradhapura had ties with the Roman-Hellenistic world to the west and with China to the east.

Abhayagiri Dagoba was built by King Abhaya in the 1st century BC. To the north is a stone slab imprinted with what is said to be a footprint of the Buddha. Other religious treasures to seek out are the 4th century **Samadhi Buddha Statue**, and **Isurumuniya Vihara** rock temple, which is noted for its sensual sculptures.

Anuradhapura Archaeological Museum contains a range of exhibits discovered on the site along with explanatory displays.

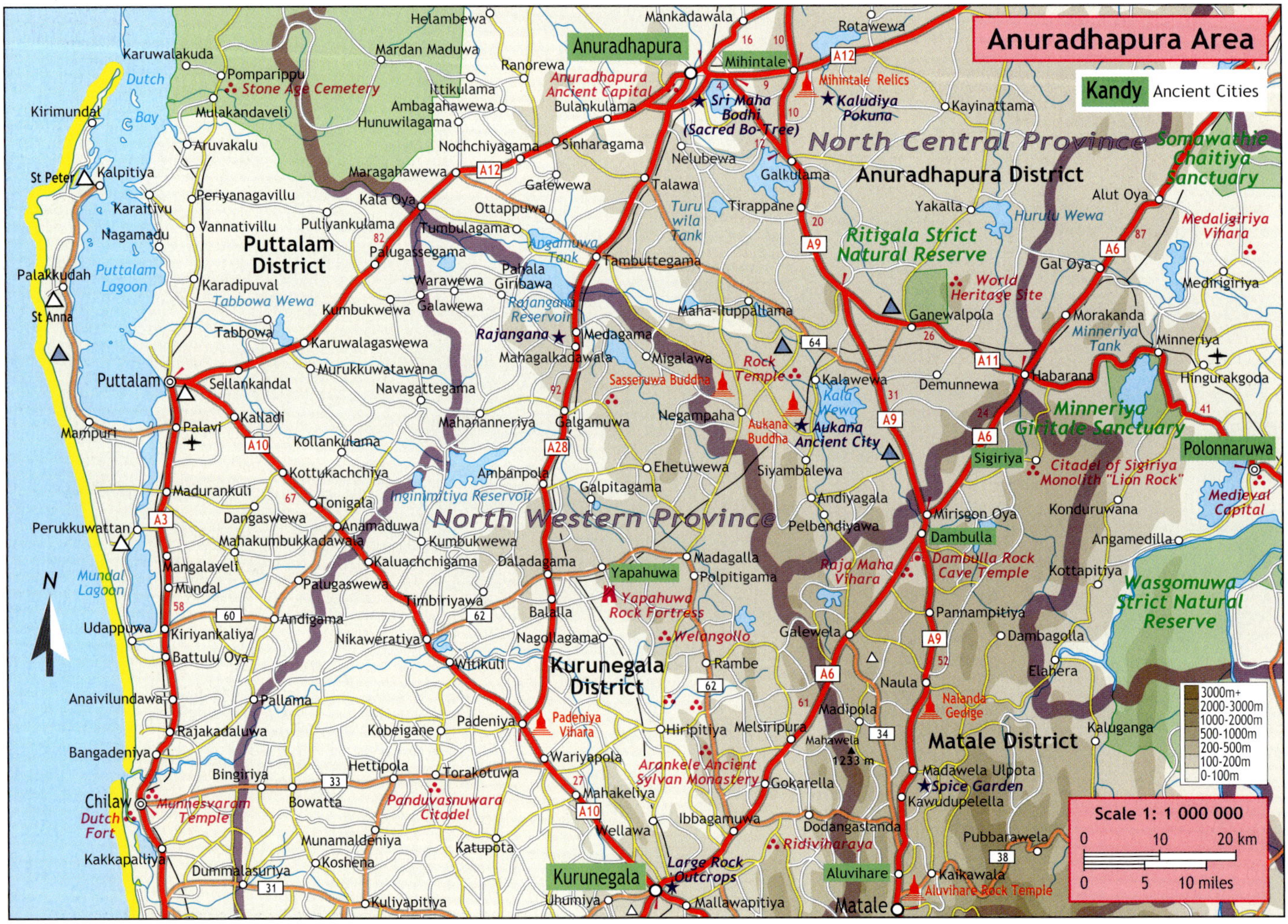

Accommodation

Polonnaruwa

Deer Park Hotel, Giritale, Polonnaruwa, tel: (027) 224 6274, fax: (027) 224 6470. Quality hotel with pool, health centre, Sri Lankan restaurant, gym and tennis.

Giritale Hotel, National Holiday Resort, Giritale, Polonnaruwa, tel: (027) 224 6311, fax: (027) 224 6068. Air-conditioned rooms, sauna, pool, fishing and boat trips.

Royal Lotus Hotel, Giritale, Polonnaruwa, tel: (027) 224 6316, fax: (027) 244 8849. Very good value, with air-conditioned rooms, pool, nature walks, wildlife safaris.

Sigiriya

The Elephant Corridor, Sigiriya, tel: (066) 223 1950, fax: (066) 223 1952, www.elephantcorridor.com Private plunge pools, four-poster beds, and views of Sigiriya fortress.

Sigiriya Village Hotel, PO Box 1, Sigiriya, tel: (066) 223 1803, fax: (066) 222 3502. This hotel has a pool, tennis and badminton courts.

Travel Tips

Although many travel agents offer day trips to the interior from the coastal resorts in the south and southeast, the area deserves far more than a whistle-stop tour. It would be much better to take at least three or four days for the treasures of the **Hill Country** and **Cultural Triangle** before heading to the coast for some rest and relaxation.

Right: *Sigiriya's elegant palaces and gardens contrast sharply with the rocky citadel that formed King Kaspaya's military stronghold. The complex dates from around 473–480AD.*

Main Attractions

This 200m (656ft) plug of rock was fortified in the late 5th century AD by Kasyapa, a patricidal usurper of the throne of Anuradhapura. Around the monolithic crag are the ramparts of the lower citadel, enclosing a complex of ruined miniature summer palaces and royal swimming pools. The staircase cut to its upper reaches has exceptional artwork including the **Sigiriya Damsels**, skimpily clad court beauties and the only secular art to have survived from the early Sinhalese kingdoms. The **Mirror Wall** preserves graffiti dating from as early as the 8th century that provided linguists with vital insight into the evolution of the Sinhalese language. Views from the summit are breathtaking. Kaspaya met an ignominious end when, after being defeated in battle by his brother Mogallana, he chose to take his own life. After Kaspaya's death Sigiriya was abandoned and fell into disuse, and its treasures were not rediscovered until the 19th century.

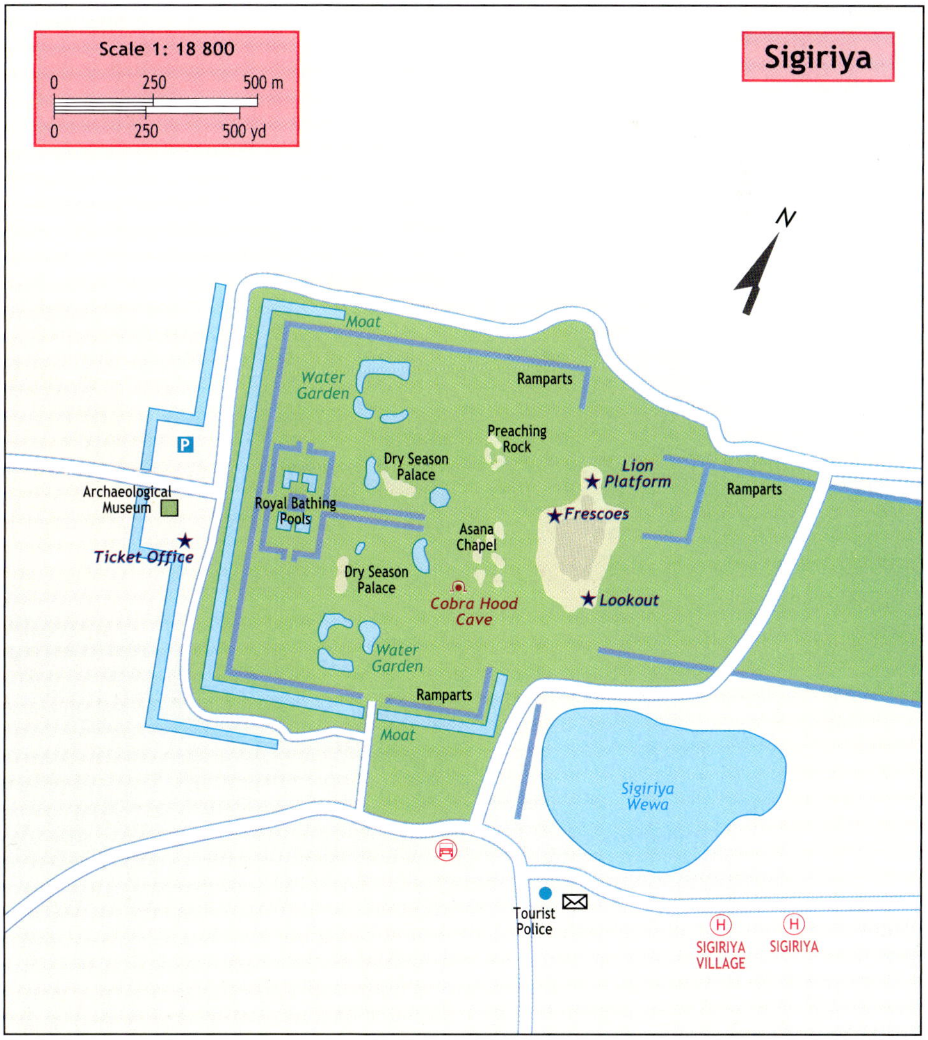

Main Attractions

Capital of Sri Lanka from the 10th to the 13th century, **Polonnaruwa's Quadrangle** guards the richest collection of ancient buildings in Sri Lanka, including the **Vatadage** (reliquary), a circular building some 18m (59ft) in diameter, with a central dagoba (shrine) which houses four seated Buddha images. The whole complex comprises more than a dozen temples and shrines.

Other highlights include a **Royal Palace** built by Parakramabahu I, the ruins of the palace of Parakramabahu I's successor, Nissanka Malla (1187–96), and the **Siva Devale**, a finely chiselled 13th-century Hindu temple. North of the city is the **Alahana Pirivena Complex**, including **Rankot Vihara**, the largest dagoba in Polonnaruwa at 55m (180ft) high, and **Gal Vihara** with its impressive and monumental Buddha statues.

The **Visitor Information Centre and Museum** displays a huge scale model of the site allowing you to get your bearings.

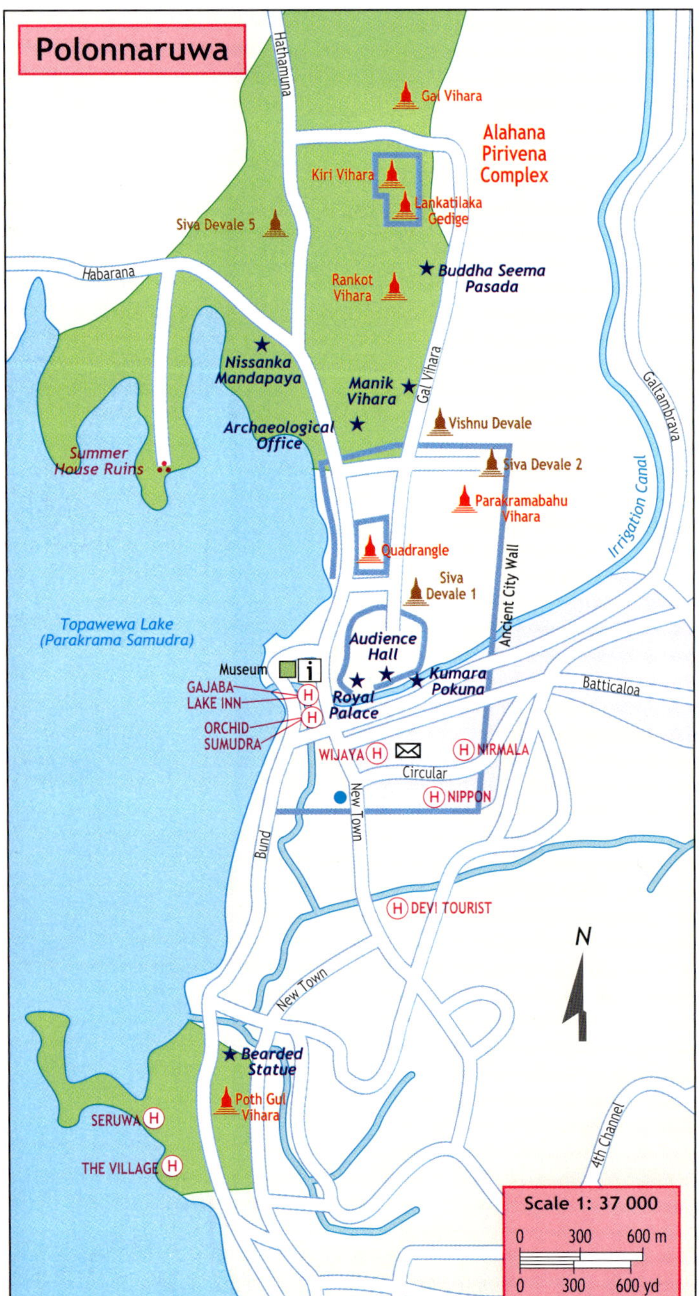

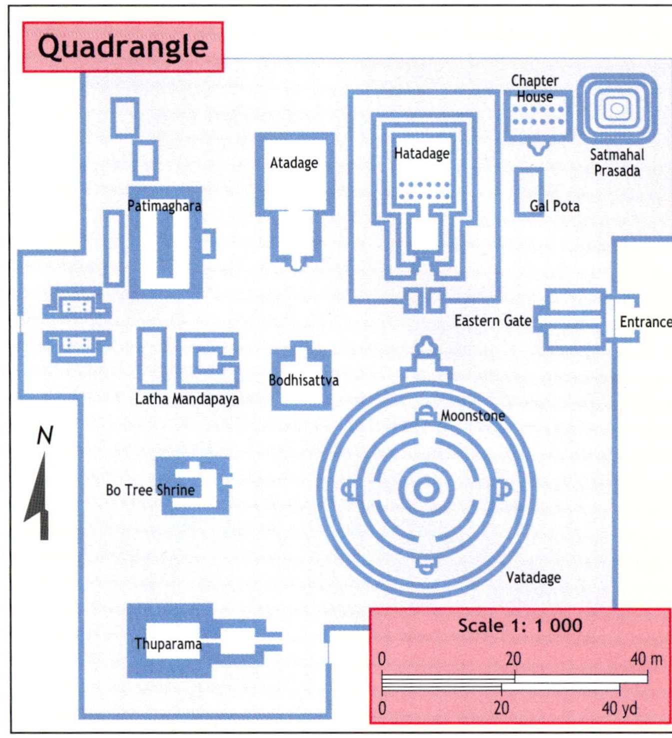

Accommodation

Anuradhapura

Tissawewa Resthouse, Old Town, Anuradhapura, tel: (025) 222 2299, fax: (025) 222 3265. Close to the lake and the archaeological site. Bikes for hire. Comfortable rooms.

Nuwarawewa Resthouse, New Town, Anuradhapura, tel: (025) 222 2565, fax: (025) 222 3265. Comfortable, low-rise colonial building with pool.

Below: *Gal Vihara at the Alahana Pirivena Complex at Polonnaruwa is one of the most important Buddhist shrines in Sri Lanka, with three colossal Buddha statues carved out of the rock face.*

Accommodation

Habarana

The Lodge, Habarana, tel: (066) 222 8316, fax: (066) 227 0046. Scenic hotel resort with 150 luxury chalets set in a lush woodland setting.

The Village, Habarana, tel: (066) 243 9046, fax: (066) 244 7087. Comfortable chalets; 106 rooms in 12 acres of lawns.

Above: *Buddhist monks live a life of simplicity and spirituality, often spending a lifetime tending to the dagoba (place of worship) in return for food and shelter.*

Main Attractions

About 13km (8 miles) east of the main Anuradhapura complex, **Mihintale** is a rock sanctuary that dates from at least 250BC and thought by many to be the birthplace of Sri Lankan Buddhism. Climb up more than 100 steps to the **Ambasthala Dagoba**, a centuries-old Buddhist shrine with an excellent view of the whole Anuradhapura site. Other features of Mihintale include 60 to 70 small caves used in the past as places of meditation by Buddhist monks.

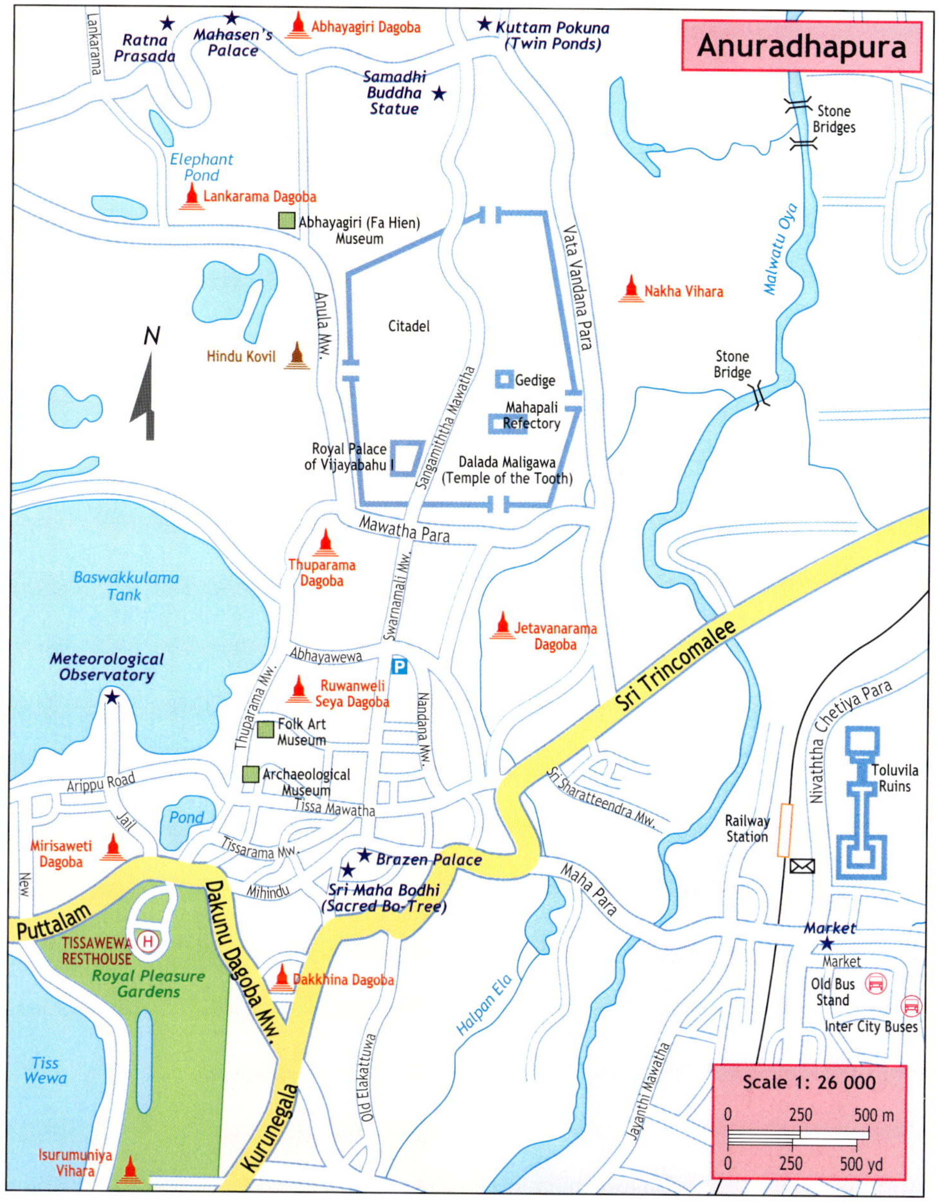

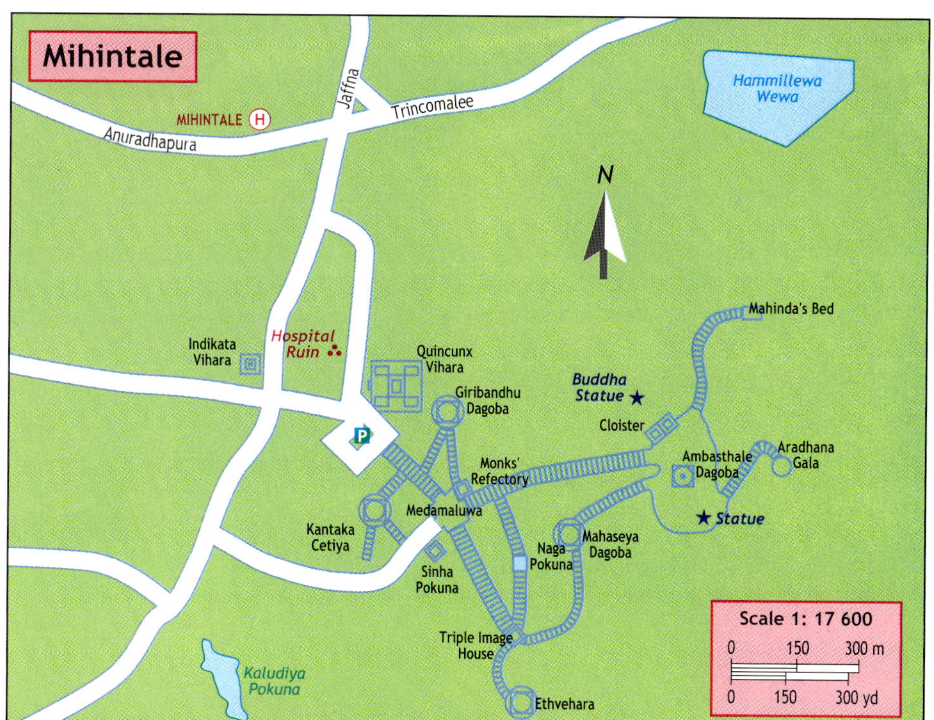

Trincomalee, East Coast and the North

The east coast, its hinterland, and the Tamil heartland of the Jaffna Peninsula are Sri Lanka's last tourism frontiers, due to the civil war of two decades. The 2004 tsunami wreaked more devastation in the east than any other part of the coast, putting back development still further. There is plenty to explore here, from historic cities that played a key role in opening Sri Lanka to the outside world, some of the Indian Ocean's last 'undiscovered' beaches, and national parks that shelter elephant, leopard and rich biodiversity. Over the next few years, assuming the political tensions ease and the infrastructure recovers, the east and north should become more popular.

Main Attractions

Trincomalee in the north and **Batticaloa** midway along the coast stand guard over two fine natural harbours, but both are rather modern towns battered by war. Admiral Lord Nelson praised the harbour of Trincomalee after a stay here and it was highly regarded by the British Royal Navy from that time. **Swami Rock** just north of Trincomalee, on the site of the ancient **Koneswara Isvaram**, is one of Sri Lanka's most important **Hindu Shrines**, despite the fact that the original was destroyed by the Portuguese soon after they arrived on the island. A stone phallus and one single pillar are all that remain of the first temple but they have a symbolic location at the summit of the rock.

A little further north, Sri Lanka's only Tamil vihara (Buddhist shrine), **Velgam Vihara** (also called **Natana Kovil** by Hindu worshippers), dates from the 2nd century AD.

In the far south of the region, **Arugam Bay** has already being rediscovered by surfers and beachcombers, and it is certainly the best place to stay on the east coast. There are several important wildlife preserves close to the town.

Jaffna in the north is the heartland of Tamil Sri Lanka. Another war-torn town with a fine fort, it is surrounded by a much dryer landscape and a coastline dotted with uninhabited islands.

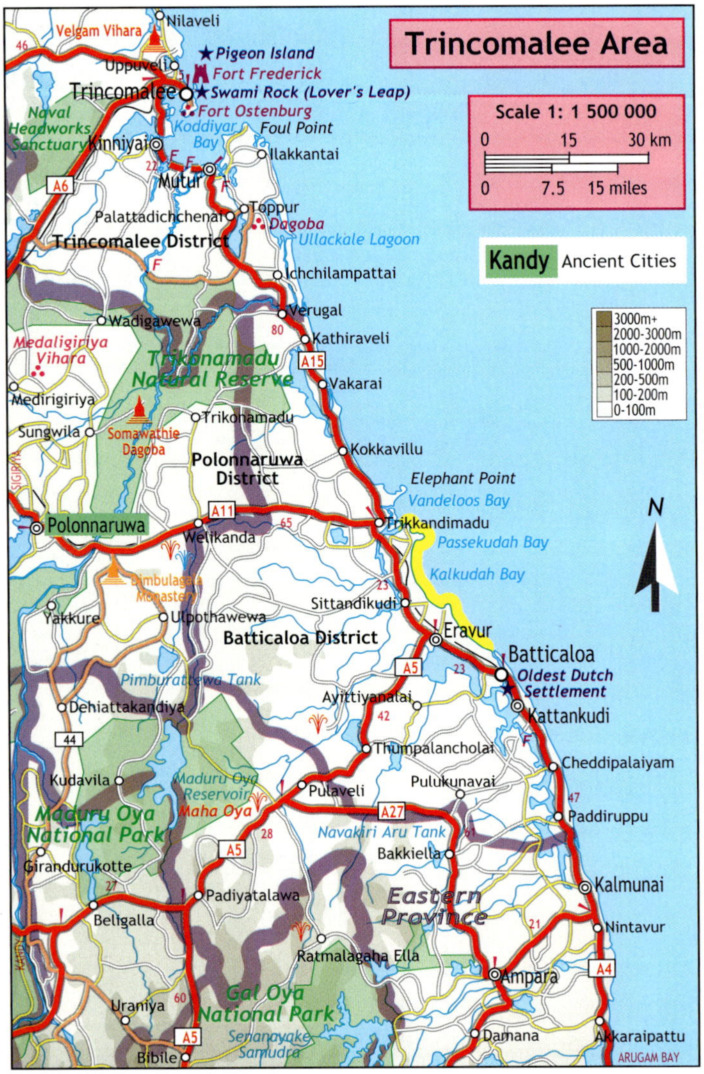

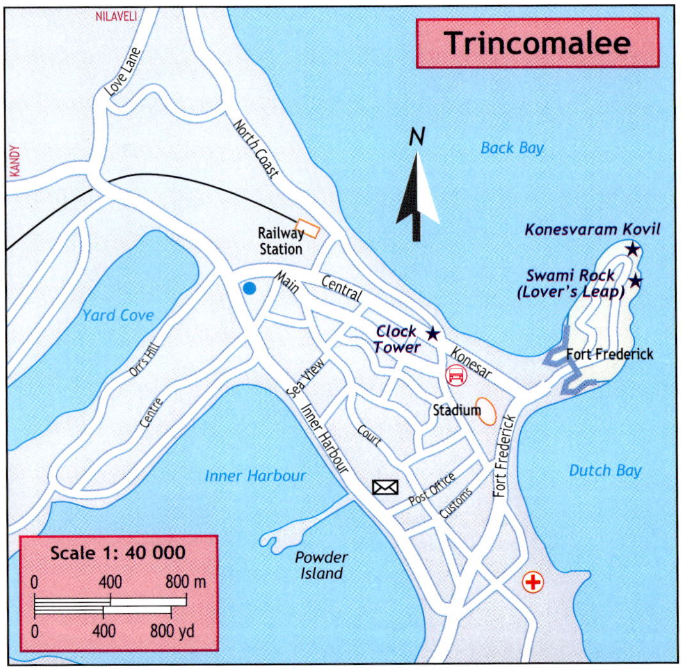

Accommodation

Trincomalee

Club Oceanic, Uppuveli, tel: (026) 222 2307. Beachside resort with a good range of activities and sandy beaches.

Welcombe Hotel, Orr's Hill, tel: (026) 222 2373, fax: (026) 222 3887, www.jetwing.net Colonial-style building; fine restaurant; 'English' pub; two separate luxury cottages.

Nilaveli Beach Hotel, 11th Milepost, Nilaveli, tel: (026) 222 2071, fax: (026) 224 8279. Some air-conditioned rooms; beach. Booking essential.

The Villa, 22 Orr's Hill Rd, tel: (026) 222 2284. Comfortable guesthouse with restaurant and en-suite rooms.

Arugam Bay

Stardust Beach Hotel, tel: (063) 224 8191, fax: (063) 906 7841. Choice of budget cabanas with shared facilities, thatched bungalows or luxury rooms, and open-air restaurant; between ocean and lagoon.

Hide Away, tel: (063) 224 8259. Four rooms with balconies overlook a garden; restaurant.

Beach Hut, Arugam Bay, tel: (063) 224 8202. Small cabanas; comfortable rooms; near beach.

Aloha Cabanas, tel: (063) 224 8379. Popular with surfers; cabanas, beach restaurant.

Above: *Arugam Bay is the perfect place to watch the Sri Lankan sunrise and is a renowned surfing bay.*

Opposite: *A local fisherman in a traditional, wooden catamaran at Nilaveli beach.*

National Parks and Protected Areas

Wilpattu National Park

Sri Lanka's largest park, Wilpattu was designated a sanctuary in 1905. Situated in the northwestern dry zone, its environments range from coastal beaches and mangroves to tropical forest. Nearly 60 water holes means abundant refreshment for the animals and birds. It protects good numbers of leopard and sloth bears but relatively few elephants. A pre-Vijayan burial ground discovered in the park bears witness to the long human history in the area.

Trikonamadu Natural Park

One of Sri Lanka's most recently created reserves, it covers 25,000 hectares of Mahaweli Ganga floodplain close to the river's mouth at Koddiyar Bay. The reserve is a crucial component in the green 'corridor' created to allow the movement of wildlife between national parks, reserves and sanctuaries. The lush grasslands of the Mahaweli Ganga valley are a rich feeding ground for the Sri Lankan lowland elephants and many species of deer.

Yala National Park

Yala is famed for relatively large numbers of leopards and its well-established elephant population. The coast forms the eastern boundary of the park, with an ever-changing vista providing excellent spots from which to view wildlife, and offers breathtaking lowland views. Kumana Mangrove Swamp is the best site for waterfowl but is difficult to get to. Other large mammals that usually put in an appearance are sloth bears, mongoose, jackal and deer.

Gal Oya National Park

Created to protect nearly 26,000 hectares around the catchment area of the Senanayake Samudra Lake, Gal Oya's deeply indented valleys and rocky peaks offer some of Sri Lanka's most dramatic landscapes. Thirty-two species of mammal have been recorded, while bird life is even richer. Of the 300 endemic birds on the island, 150 species have been noted here. You can take boat trips on the lake to view the shoreline birds and animals.

Maduru Oya National Park

Protecting Buddhist ruins dating back to the 6th century BC, Maduru Oya was designated a national park in 1983 and its 59,000 hectares protect important populations of Sri Lankan primates including the slender loris (a small nocturnal mammal about the size of a chipmunk), toque monkey and the grey langur. The extensive wetlands are also particularly popular with crocodile, which are reported to be abundant in number, and water monitors.

Uda Walawe National Park

Arguably the best place in Sri Lanka for elephant-watching, Uda Walawe is a dry zone park and protects important stands of ancient trees including large teak specimens, but vast tracts of land cleared before area was protected in 1972 means that it's much easier to see the animals than in other parks. Other large animals to look out for are sambur, boar and buffalo, but Uda Walawe is also famed for its bird life including several raptor species.

Peak Wilderness Sanctuary

Sri Lanka's third largest sanctuary covers the land surrounding Adam's Peak Mountain, in the heart of Hill Country. The Sanctuary protects some dramatic upland scenery, with steep-sided mountain slopes, dense jungle and treacherous rivers and streams that have carved magnificent waterfalls through the greenery. This is the birthplace of several of the island's major rivers and the undisturbed endemic flora makes it one of the most important repositories for avifauna, butterflies and larger animals.

Giant's Tank Sanctuary

One of the largest of the ancient tanks or reservoirs cut by the Kings of Sri Lanka to irrigate the lands of the dry zone, this 3800-ha lake makes a reliable water hole for the wildlife of the northeast. The tank is a habitat for numerous birds, attracting land and marine species, but is also close to the Madhu Road Sanctuary whose animals view the tank as an emergency bolt hole in times of drought. This sanctuary has been little visited because it lies at the edge of the war zone.

Madhu Road Sanctuary

Protected since 1968 and occupying a 26,000-hectare tract in the north close to Palk Bay and Giant's Tank, Madhu Road Sanctuary is one of Sri Lanka's few truly dry zone sanctuaries and acts as a corridor extension of virgin dry monsoon forest north from Wilpattu National Park for the elephant populations of the northeast. This area, particularly around the Catholic town of Madhu, was the site of refugee settlement from the Jaffna Peninsula and of several Sri Lankan army operations during the troubles.

Wasgomuwa Strict Natural Reserve

Wasgomuwa Strict Natural Reserve protects low-lying flood plains between the Mahaweli Ganga and one of its tributaries. This rich grassland is favoured by a population of elephants, known as 'swamp elephants' because they thrive in the ever-changing water levels. The Sri Lankan sloth bear is one of fourteen carnivores to live in the park. Wasgomuwa almost links with Trikonamadu Natural Park – part of an attempt to create a wildlife corridor for Sri Lankan wild fauna.

Victoria Randenigala Rantambe Sanctuary

A few miles east of Kandy River, Victoria Randenigala Rantambe Sanctuary incorporates large expanses of water created by two hydroelectric dams surrounded by dense monsoon forest. The flora is representative of the transition zones between wet and dry regions and is one of the most varied of any national park on Sri Lanka. It is home to macaques, elephant, leopard, civet and wild boar, plus an array of birds and reptiles. The stupa of Raja Vihara in the sanctuary is the oldest on Sri Lanka.

National Parks and Protected Areas

National Route Planner

Legend and Scale

National road Nationalstraße Route nationale	
Main road Hauptstraße Route principale	
Secondary road Nebenstraße Route secondaire	
Track Sandpiste Piste/Sentier	
Distance in kilometres Entfernung in Kilometern Distance en kilomètres	19 15
Railway Eisenbahn Chemin de fer	
Provincial boundary Provinzgrenze Frontière provinciale	
District boundary Bezirksgrenze Frontière de district	
Route number Routennummer Numéro de route	A1 42
Airport Flughafen Aéroport	INT Other
City Großstadt Ville	COLOMBO
Major Town Kreisstadt Ville importante	Moratuwa
Town Stadt Ville secondaire	Panadura
Large village Größere Ortschaft Grand village	Gampaha
Village Dorf Village	Seeduwa

Viewpoint Aussichtspunkt Point de vue	Ella Gap
Place of interest Sehenswürdigkeit Endroit à visiter	Clock Tower
Water feature Gewässer Eau	River Dam
Waterfall Wasserfall Chute d'eau	Elgin
Reef Riff Récif	Coral Gardens
Province name Provinzname Nom de la province	Western Province
District name Bezirksname Nom du District	Matara District
Ruin Ruine Ruines	Pubbarama
Lighthouse Leuchtturm Phare	
Cave Höhle Grotte	Belilena
Hindu Temple Hindutempel Temple Hindou	Hindu Kovil
Buddhist Temple Buddhistentempel Temple Bouddhiste	Nakha Vihara
Monastery Kloster Monastère	Malvatta Monastery
Fort Burg Château	Dutch Fort
Peak in metres Höhe in Metern Altitude (en mètres)	Haycock 661 m

Museum Museum Museu	Dutch Period Museum
Embassy Botschaft Ambassade	Spain
Bank Bank Banque	Bank of Ceylon HQ
Church Kirche Église	St Peter's
Mosque Moschee Mosquée	Grand Mosque
Nature reserve and park Naturschutzgebiet und Park Réserve naturelle et parc	Horton Plains National Park
Beach Strand Plage	
Ferry route Fährverbindung Ferry/bac	F
Golf course Golfplatz Terrain de golf	Nuwawra Eliya Golf Club
Hot spring Heiße Quelle Fontaine chaud	Hot Springs
Spring Quelle Fontaine	Spring
Main road Hauptstraße Route principale	Peradeniya
Road Straße Route	Raja Veediya
Wall Mauer Remparts	
Building of interest Interessantes Bauwerke Edifice intéressant	World Trade Centre

Parking area Parkplatz Parking	P
Restaurant Restaurant Restaurant	R Restaurant
Hotel (selected) Hotel (Auswahl) Hôtel (sélectionné)	H CARLTON
Hospital Krankenhaus Hôpital	General Hospital
Post office Postamt Bureau de poste	
Information centre Auskunftsbüro Centre d'information	i
Bus terminus Busbahnhof Terminus d'autobus	Inter City Buses
Built-up area Wohngebiet Agglomération	
Library Bibliothek Bibliothèque	
Shopping Centre Einkaufszentrum Centre commercial	S
Gate Tor Porte	Old Gate
University Universität Université	University of Kelaniya
College College College	Trinity College
Safe bathing beach Badestrand Baignade autorisée	
Water sport Wassersport Sports nautiques	W
Snorkelling Schnorcheln Plongée avec tuba	

Kandy Ancient Cities

Scale 1: 400 000 — 0, 10, 20 miles / 0, 20, 30 km

The Jaffna Islands

Like the pincers of a crab, two groups of islands stretch out towards each other into the waters of the Palk Strait. This narrow channel is the physical divide between Sri Lanka and India but has proved no boundary to the transfer of ideas and people between the two regions. In ancient times, the Kings of Jaffna harvested pearls from the shallow waters around the islands that were traded around the known world. The money earned built fantastic palaces and paid for the cutting of the first irrigation tanks. The archipelago of small islands in the Palk Strait were off limits for many years (see Travel Tips).

Main Attractions

The islands have a scattering of colonial forts and temples. **Nainativu** is one of the smallest populated islands and one of the 16 sacred places in the Mahavamsa Buddhist chronicles. These offer a full and fascinating account of the development of the religion on Sri Lanka, and the lives of the kings who championed the religion and promoted it to their people. There's a stone said to bear the footprint of Buddha at Nagadipa Vihara on Nainativu, but though the site has ancient antecedents, the temple itself is a 1950s rebuild.

Delft Island is the most interesting, with the remains of a **Portuguese castle** (later taken over by the Dutch) and small herds of wild horses that may be the descendants of Portuguese steeds. Often horses were let loose on small islands to feed after the long journey from Europe and they were probably forgotten when the Portuguese left in the wake of the Dutch arrival.

Further south, **Mannar Island** (connected to the mainland by man-made causeway) has yet another small **Portuguese Fort**, Sao Jorge, at the easternmost point. Mannar is the eastern terminus of **Adam's Bridge** or Rama's Bridge, a string of rocks, shoals and islets stretching 30km (18miles) across Palk Strait that's covered by 1.2m (4ft) of water at high tide. This is considered the last land connection between India and Sri Lanka and a Hindu legend tells of how Rama used the bridge to rescue his wife from the demon Ravana and take her back to India. The popular Ramayana dance - often seen in traditional dance shows around the island and at major hotels - tells the story of this epic tale of good versus evil (Rama versus Ravana) and of a powerful true love that conquers the dark side. See it if you can.

Above: *Turtles are now being protected at sites around the island.*
Below: *Traditional sailing craft still ply the shallow waters around Jaffna.*

Travel Tips

Avoid buying goods made from ivory, turtle shell, or reptile skin of any kind. Local vendors may assure you that such wild animal products are legal in Sri Lanka or are made from species which are not endangered. This is unlikely to be true (there are no snake or other reptile farms in Sri Lanka) and your new purchases will be confiscated by customs on your return home.

Islands in the Palk Strait: When this atlas went to press it was possible to visit most of them by boat from Jaffna but visitors should check in advance whether this is possible.

Peace talks between the government and the LTTE are currently underway, but keep in mind that travel restrictions may be imposed at short notice if the situation changes. Always check that access is still possible before travelling.

A
B
C
D
1
2
3
4
5
3000m+
2000-3000m
1000-2000m
500-1000m
200-500m
100-200m
0-100m
N
Palk Strait
Karaitivu
Karainagar
Moolai
74
JAFFNA
Kalapoomy
Hammenhiel Fort
Eluvaitivu
Urundi Fort
Kayts
Karampan
Analaitivu
Analaitivu
Narantanai
Saravanai
Suruvil
Velanai
Nagadipa Vihara
Irruppiddi
Kayts
Nainativu
Naga Pooshani Ammal Kovil
Punkudutivu
Nainativu
Punkudutivu
Delft Channel
Wild Horses
Periyaturai
Maveliturai
Portuguese Castle
Vediresan Koddai
Delft
31
Kachchativu
INDIAN OCEAN
Adam's Bridge
Mannar Island
Talaimannar
37
Pesalai
Nadukkuda
Erukkulampiddi
ANURADHAPURA
35

Jaffna District

Jaffna and its surrounding district is the heartland of the distinctive Tamil culture. The flat, arid peninsula encloses a complex of huge lagoons, and is connected to the mainland by two narrow causeways at Elephant Pass – which carries the main highway and was the scene of frequent, fierce fighting between LTTE and government forces – and Chundikkulam, where a poorly maintained road runs through the Chundikkulam Bird Sanctuary, a haven for numerous endemic bird species. This region awaits its inclusion on the mainstream tourist trail but the continued security problems have dampened a rise in confidence that followed the declaration of a ceasefire in 2002.

Main Attractions

The city of Jaffna, also known as Yaalpaanam, might be a place for all humanity to come and view the futility of war. Ravaged buildings bear witness to the years of fighting. The city's most prominent building is the star-shaped fort built by the Dutch and still garrisoned and heavily defended by the Sri Lankan Army. A small dusty collection of pre-colonial and colonial relics is on view at the **Archaeological Museum**. By contrast **Kandaswamy Kovil** is Sri Lanka's most spectacularly colourful Hindu temple, dominated by three towers covered by a riot of carved and painted deities and demons. The ancient capital of the Kings of Jaffna was situated at **Kantharodai** in the heart of the peninsula. Archaeologists have discovered that the dynasty had contact with ancient Rome, Mesopotamia and China. Just a short distance from the city is the northern-most town in Sri Lanka, **Point Pedro**, its coastline yet to be discovered by the outside world.

Above: *The beaches of the east coast are some of the least spoiled in Sri Lanka.*
Left: *Hindu festivals always involve beautifully prepared offerings of food.*

Accommodation

Ashok Hotel, 3 Clock Tower Rd, tel: (021) 222 4336. Jaffna's best; 32 air-conditioned rooms, restaurant, pool, bars, room service. Booking essential.
Harbour View Hotel, Keerimalai Rd, tel: (021) 259 5737. Restaurant, bar.
Subash Tourist Hotel, 15 Victoria Rd, tel: (021) 222 3228. Affordable; two restaurants.
Yarl Beach Inn, 8 Old Park Rd, Jaffna, tel: (021) 222 5490. Four quiet rooms (two air conditioned); friendly owners.

A
B
C
D
1
2
3
4
5
3000m+
2000-3000m
1000-2000m
500-1000m
200-500m
100-200m
0-100m
N
Naguleswarm Shiva Temple
Kankesanturai
Keerimalai
Valveddittuarai
Valalai
Point Pedro
Tumpalai
Nelliadi
Puloli
Palali
Udduppidi
Vasavilan
Tellippalai
Karaveddi
Vallipuram
Manalkadu
Dutch Church
Achchuveli
Pandattarippu
Chankanai
Chunnakam
Vallipura Alvar Kovil
Puttur
Kantharodai
Nilavarai Tidal Well
Varani
Ampan
addukoddai
Manippay
Neerveli
Urampiram
Jaffna District
Arali
Nallur Kandaswamy Temple
Sarasalai
Nagar Kovil
Bay of Bengal
Anaicoddai
Kokkuvil
Kodikamam
Mirusuvil
Kudarappu
Jaffna
Dutch Fort
Navatkuli
Kaitadi
Chavakachcheri
A9
Eluthumadduval
Archaeological Museum
Kachchai
Lagoon
Allaippiddi
A32
55
Kilali
Dutch Fort
Mandaitivu
Pallai
Chempiyanpattu
Mandaitivu
Kalmunai
Aliavalai
Tanmakkeni
Soranpattu
Kavutarimunai
Mulliyan
Iyakachchi
Chundikkulam Bird Sanctuary
Jaffna Lagoon
Elephant Pass
Vannankulam
29
33
Saltern Siding
Cheddiyakurichchi
Pooneryn
St Anthony
Uriyan
Chundikkulam
Palaitivu
Kandavalai
Nallur
69
Palk Bay
Nawaladi
Sempankundu
Murasumoddai
Periyaparantan
Paranthan
Velikkandal
Palavi
Uruthirapuram
Theravil Aru
Kilinochchi
Devil's Point
Vaddakkachchi
A32
Kilinochchi District
Ponnayeli
Valappadu
Veravil
Chunnavil
Theravilkulam
Kunchukkulam
Erumaitivu
Kiranchi
Iranamadu
Kokkavil (old)
Manniyakulam
37
Kakkativu
Terumurikandi
Udayarkattu Kulam
Pallavarayankaddu
Akkarayan Kulam
Iranamadu Tank
Kumulamunai
Mandekal Aru
Kokkavil
Iranativu
Murikandy
Karlyale Nagapaduwan
Mullaittivu District
Mutaliyarkulam
Padinaddampore
A9
Northern Province
Muthuaiyankadu Kulam
Uyilankulam
Vellankulam
Panikkankulam
Terankandai
90
Pali Aru
Tunukkai
Olumadu
48
Karuppaddamurippu
Mundampiddi
Vadakadu
Mallavi
Vannivilankulam
Mankulam
Katkidanku
Kurunthankulam
Iluppaikkadavai
Oddankulam
Appakkuttikinattadi
Parappukkal
Vavuni Kulam
Kalliyadi
Attimoddai
Iramiyankulam
Kanakarayankulam
37
Madhu Road Sanctuary
Panankamam
MANNAR
VAVUNIYA
MULLAITTIVU

Mullaittivu District

The Mullaittivu District cuts a swathe across the northern tip of mainland Sri Lanka. Among the dominant features are several tanks that drain west into Palk Bay, north into Jaffna Lagoon or east to the Indian Ocean. The long eastern coastline is dotted with small fishing villages. Often at the front line between government and LTTE forces, much of the indigenous population was displaced during the troubles and land mines laid across the countryside, so the latent tourist potential has never been harnessed. This coastline was particularly hard hit by the 2004 tsunami, with many thousands dead, and Tamils complain that aid has been slow to arrive.

Travel Tips

Travel to the northern areas should be undertaken with caution. Fields of uncleared land mines lie all across the region and constant military and insurgency activities up until the ceasefire of 2002 means that there is little tourism infrastructure. You are currently advised to take official advice (try the UK Foreign Office website, www.fco.gov.uk) before entering the area.

Climate
Sri Lanka has a tropical climate with no cool season and average temperatures of 27°C (80.6°F) rising to a maximum of 35°C (95°F) along the coast.
Always carry insect repellent and sun screen to protect against possible insect bites and sunburn.

Above: *Nilaveli Beach is one of the finest on the east coast but the tourism infrastructure is still recovering from the 2004 tsunami.*
Below: *Sri Lanka's bird population enjoys some of the excellent coastal and lagoon habitats with vast mangrove swamps for protection against predators.*

Useful Contacts

For further information concerning the peace process, visit the official government website www.peaceinsrilanka.org or the Tamil website www.eelam.com

Main Attractions

The district capital **Mullaittivu** was once a characterful town with a mainly Catholic population, but has been racked by years of intermittent violence. It made a living from fishing before the troubles and the native population were only just beginning to return in numbers from camps in India when the tsunami struck in December 2004. The town was decimated, with many lives lost. A bronze statue by an American sculptor commemorating the disaster was donated to the town.

Inland from the town is **Nanthi Kadal Lagoon**, a brackish environment, while the **Chundikula and Kokkilai Bird Sanctuary** sits in the far south of the district around the **Kokkilai Lagoon**. This will be an excellent location for migratory and native wading birds when the area opens up to tourism. Bring your binoculars to make the best of these conditions.

A
B
C
D
1
2
3
4
5
3000m+
2000-3000m
1000-2000m
500-1000m
200-500m
100-200m
0-100m
N
INDIAN OCEAN
31
Kariyalvayal
Chalai
KILINOCHCHI
Putumattalan
A35
57
Valayanmadam
Karaiyamullivaikal
Puthukkudiyiruppu
Nanthi Kadal Lagoon
F
Mullaittivu
Pirappuvedduvan
Per Aru
Chilavattai
Katkulam
Mulliyawalai
Tanniyuttu
Keridamadu
Mullaittivu District
A34
Kulumurippu
Alampil
Oddusuddan
Chemmalai
Kodalikallu
Kumulamunai
MANKULAM
Tannimurippu Kulam
Tanduvan
Vavuniya District
Nedunkeni
Kokkilai Lagoon
Kokkuttoduval
39
Chundikula & Kokkilai Bird Sanctuary

Mannar District

Although the Mannar region is one of the least known and least visited districts in Sri Lanka, it played an important role in Sri Lanka's development, principally because of that most precious aquatic wealth producer - pearls. The region pretty much lost out on tourism revenue during the internecine troubles of the 1980s and 1990s. In fact it became a place of refuge for displaced residents of Jaffna and points further north. However its range of historic, religious and natural attractions should draw visitors once the north fully opens up. This very much depends on the progress of peace talks between the Sri Lankan government, the rebel LTTE forces and Tamil political leaders.

Main Attractions

Mannar town sits on the island of the same name set just offshore from the mainland and linked to it by a short modern causeway. The most prominent feature is a colonial fort completed by the Portuguese in 1560 and maintained by the Dutch, but it had been an important port long before this period.

Mannar Island is the largest and most westerly part of the feature known as **Adam's Bridge** or Rama's Bridge, a string of low-lying islands (mostly submerged during high tide) that reach across the narrow strait to India.

South of Mannar Island lie Sri Lanka's famed **Pearl Beds**. For generations throughout the reign of the Sri Lankan kings of antiquity - even as early as the Hellenistic and Roman Empires - the pearls were harvested here and shipped around the world and their quality was highly regarded. However, the industry died out about a hundred years ago and is no longer practised in the region. Today this is one of the few places around the shores to find the dugong or sea cow. Many think that sightings of this large marine mammal probably gave rise to the myth of the mermaid.

Inland the district offers a range of dry zone environments from jungle to rice paddy. The vast **Giant's Tank** (ancient artificial reservoir) is now a pro tected sanctuary for a variety of bird and animal life, along with the **Madhu Road Sanctuary**.

The tiny town of Madhu is at the heart of a mainly Catholic area and **Our Lady of the Holy Rosary** is one of the island's primary Christian pilgrimage sites. Since Catholicism was established on the island in the post-colonial era this site has been known for its miracles - curing blindness and delivering people from snake bites.

Useful Contacts

Eco Team 14 1st Lane, Gothami Road, Colombo, tel/fax: (011) 553 3330, www.srilankaecotourism.com offers a range of off-the-rack tours or can arrange bespoke packages combining adventure and nature tours or eco- and agrotourism activities.

Top: *The white-bellied eagle spends most of its day hunting from the water's edge, and is one of Sri Lanka's main avian predator species.*

Left: *Basket weaving is one of the major handicrafts of the island and the objects produced make excellent souvenirs.*

A
B
C
D
29
41
37
1
2
3
4
5
Pesalai
Nadukkuda
Erukkulampiddi
Toddaveli
Malivadi
Mannar
Mantota
Talladi
A14
Vankalai
Mathotam
Uyilankulam
Adampan
Adankulam
Tirukketiswaram
Kalliyadi
KILINOCHCHI
Attimoddai
Vidattaltivu
Pallamadu
Madhu Road Sanctuary
Nay Aru
Periyamadhu
Mannar District
Palampiddi
Our Lady of the Holy Rosary
Madhu
Giant's Tank
Giant's Tank Sanctuary
Murunkan
Nanaddan
Aruvi Aru
Arippu
Veppankulam
Kovitkulam
43
Madhu Road
Paraiyanalankulam
Periyakaddo
44
VAVUNIYA
Periyakunchukkulam
Silavattura
Kondaichchi
Gulf of Mannar
Pearl Banks
Kal Aru
Periyamurippu
Karadikkuli
Marichchukkaddi
Mullikkulam
Paymadu
Kudremalai Point
Mahawilachchiya
Kaaradumunai
Modaragam Aru
Wilpattu National Park
Mahawilachchiya Tank
Pallugaturai
Portugal Bay
Karaitivu
Helambewa
N
Mardan Maduwa
Karuwalakuda
Ranorewa
Pomparippu
Ittikulama
Stone Age Cemetery
Mulakandaveli
Ambagahawewa
Dutch Bay
Pan Ela
Kirimundal
Hunuwilagama
Aruvakalu
Nochchiyagama
ANURADHAPURA
PUTTALAM
3000m+
2000-3000m
1000-2000m
500-1000m
200-500m
100-200m
0-100m

Anuradhapura District

Anchored by the huge and impressive ancient capital of Anuradhapura, the district encompasses many important religious and historical sites plus tracts of protected forest that mean it's very worthwhile to spend a few days exploring. The rulers of Anuradhapura held sway over this whole region and their patronage allowed the building of magnificent Buddhist works of art and monumental civic structures, including several large tanks or reservoirs that captured water from rivers flowing from the hill country to the south, and guaranteed water for irrigation in a region that forms part of Sri Lanka's 'dry zone'. These tanks remain invaluable to modern farmers.

Main Attractions

Once you have visited the main sites of the Anuradhapura district, take time to enjoy the Loha Prasada, once home to a community of over 100 monks who were sworn to attend to the wellbeing of the Sacred Bo Tree. The building was once decorated with silver and gems. The remains of the once-glorious Royal Palace lie in ruins north of the Thuparama Vatadage, but some of the serene tranquillity of the Royal Pleasure Gardens can still be felt, where at the height of its beauty some 35 hectares was preened with fountains and ponds. About 23km (15 miles) west of Habarana, off the main A11 highway (*see* map, page 42), **Ritigala Forest Monastery** was founded in the 1st century BC on the site from where, according to Hindu tradition, Hanuman sprang back to India to tell Rama that his wife Sita had been safely recovered from kidnappers. The surrounding forest is rich in flora and fauna.

Occupying a 1100km^2 (425 sq mile) tract of shoreline and jungle stretching inland across Puttalam District (*see* page 40–41) into Anuradhapura District, **Wilpattu** is Sri Lanka's largest national park. On the northeastern fringes of the park is **Tantirimale**, a Buddhist temple founded at the site where one of the eight samplings to be cut from the original Bo tree of Anuradhapura was planted. The temple contains three monumental Buddha statues while the museum on site displays rare idolatrous images created before Buddhism was established on Sri Lanka.

There are also major Buddhist treasures in the southern tip of the district. The 5th-century standing statue of Buddha at **Aukana** stands 12m (40ft) high and reaches a width of 3m (10ft) at the shoulder. Just west is another at **Sasseruva** that would have rivalled it in size and quality; however, this was never finished.

Above: *The Isurumuniya Vihara is noted for its sensual friezes of embracing couples.*
Below: *The Kuttam Pokuna were used by monks of Anuradhupura's monasteries.*

Travel Tips

The following New Holland Titles will be invaluable companions for wildlife spotting and identification:
Birds of Sri Lanka by Gehan Silva Wijeyeratne, Deepal Warakagoda and T. S. U. de Zylva (ISBN 1859745113) provides invaluable information of the species you can find on the island, with helpful hints of calls, natural environments, breeding patterns and the plumage variations of the sexes.
Snakes & Other Reptiles of Sri Lanka by Indraneil Das (ISBN 1843309238). The text indicates size, colour and suitable geographical habitats to enable you to seek out these usually shy creatures.
Mammals of South-East Asia by Charles M Francis (ISBN 1859745075). The author offers lots of helpful background information about the lifestyle and habits of these often elusive large creatures, including the leopard, the lemur and the elephant.

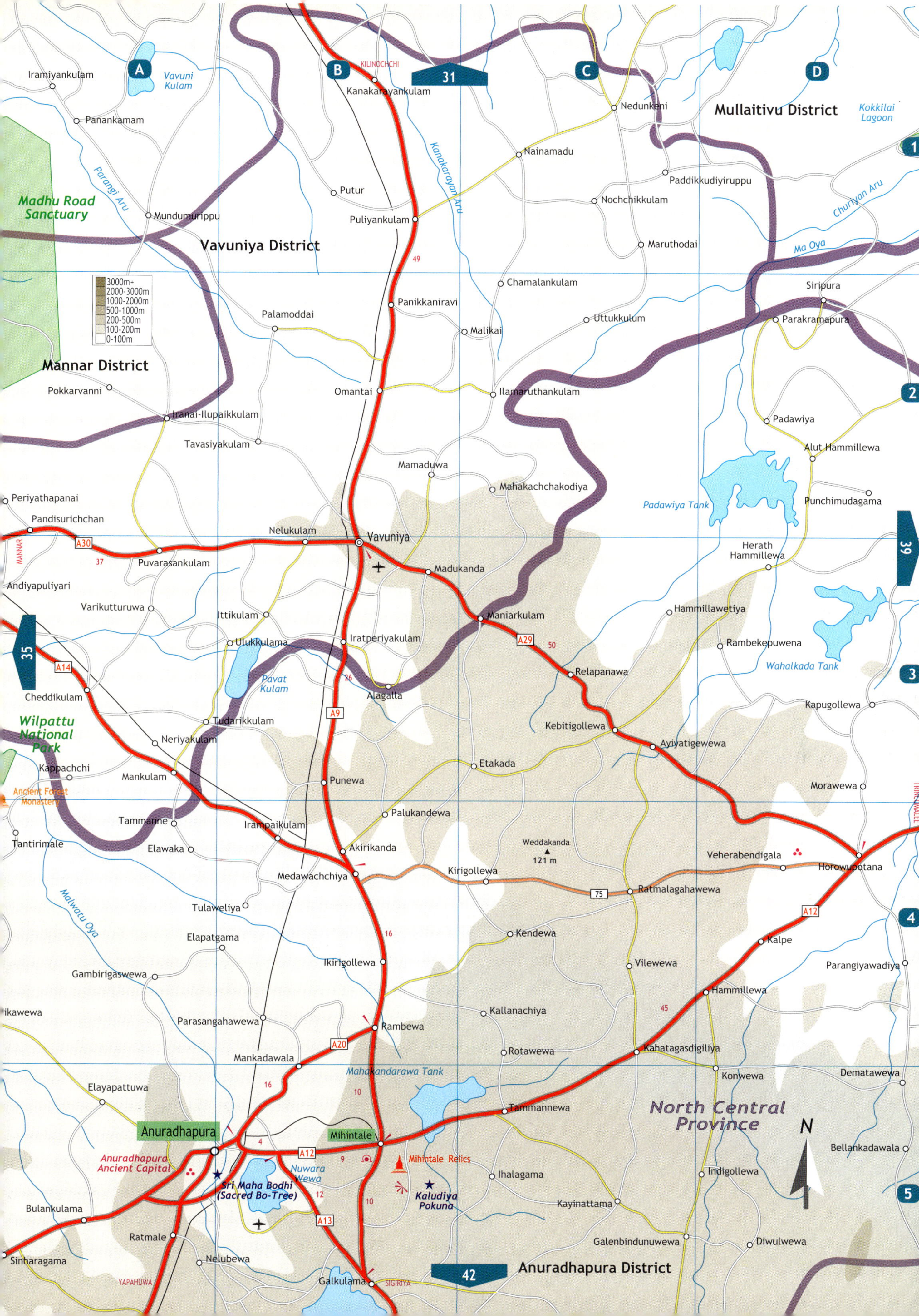
A
B
C
D
31
KILINOCHCHI
Iramiyankulam
Vavuni Kulam
Kanakarayankulam
Nedunkeni
Mullaitivu District
Kokkilai Lagoon
1
Panankamam
Nainamadu
Parangi Aru
Kanakarayan Aru
Paddikkudiyiruppu
Putur
Nochchikkulam
Madhu Road Sanctuary
Mundumurippu
Puliyankulam
Churiyan Aru
Vavuniya District
Maruthodai
Ma Oya
49
3000m+
2000-3000m
1000-2000m
500-1000m
200-500m
100-200m
0-100m
Chamalankulam
Siripura
Panikkaniravi
Parakramapura
Palamoddai
Uttukkulum
Malikai
Mannar District
2
Pokkarvanni
Omantai
Ilamaruthankulam
Iranai-Ilupaikkulam
Padawiya
Tavasiyakulam
Alut Hammillewa
Mamaduwa
Mahakachchakodiya
Periyathapanai
Punchimudagama
Padawiya Tank
Pandisurichchan
Nelukulam
Vavuniya
Herath Hammillewa
39
MANNAR
A30
37
Puvarasankulam
Madukanda
Andiyapuliyari
Varikutturuwa
Hammillawetiya
Ittikulam
Maniarkulam
Ulukkulama
Iratperiyakulam
A29
50
Rambekepuwena
35
Wahalkada Tank
A14
Pavat Kulam
26
Relapanawa
3
Cheddikulam
Alagalla
A9
Kapugollewa
Wilpattu National Park
Tudarikkulam
Kebitigollewa
Neriyakulam
Ayiyatigewewa
Etakada
Kappachchi
Mankulam
Punewa
Morawewa
Ancient Forest Monastery
TRINCOMALEE
Palukandewa
Tammanne
Irampaikulam
Weddakanda
121 m
Tantirimale
Elawaka
Akirikanda
Veherabendigala
Horowupotana
Medawachchiya
Kirigollewa
75
Ratmalagahawewa
Malwatu Oya
Tulaweliya
A12
4
16
Kendewa
Elapatgama
Kalpe
Ikirigollewa
Vilewewa
Parangiyawadiya
Gambirigaswewa
Hammillewa
ikawewa
45
Kallanachiya
Parasangahawewa
Rambewa
Rotawewa
A20
Mankadawala
Kahatagasdigiliya
Mahakandarawa Tank
Konwewa
Dematawewa
16
10
Elayapattuwa
Tammannewa
North Central Province
Anuradhapura
4
Mihintale
N
A12
9
Mihintale Relics
Bellankadawala
Anuradhapura Ancient Capital
Sri Maha Bodhi (Sacred Bo-Tree)
Nuwara Wewa
Ihalagama
Indigollewa
12
Kaludiya Pokuna
10
5
Bulankulama
Kayinattama
A13
Ratmale
Galenbindunuwewa
Diwulwewa
Sinharagama
Nelubewa
42
Anuradhapura District
YAPAHUWA
Galkulama
SIGIRIYA

Trincomalee District

With the finest natural harbour for hundreds of miles in any direction, Trincomalee drew the attention of European navigators as early as the 17th century. Occupied by the Portuguese, it later changed hands from the Dutch to the French and finally to the British in the wars of the 18th century. From 1795, it became one of the British Empire's most important Asian seaports, and during World War II it was the nerve centre of the Allies for Southeast Asia. The region has not fared well since independence, however. An LTTE stronghold, it was starved of investment, which stunted industry, and the countryside was abandoned as the population sought refuge from the fighting.

Main Attractions

Trincomalee, or Trinco as it is normally known, is a mainly post-colonial city. Just north of the town, a modern temple stands atop **Swami Rock**, on the site of the ancient **Koneswara Isvaram**, one of Sri Lanka's most important Hindu shrines, at the tip of a jutting peninsula. On Fridays, it is crowded with Hindu worshippers.

Uppuveli is the closest beach to Trinco, but **Nilaveli**'s 4km (2.5-mile) stretch of sand ten kilometres or so further north makes the best base. Just offshore is **Pigeon Island**, habitat for the rare blue rock pigeon and an excellent scuba diving and snorkelling site.

Between the two resorts is 2nd century AD **Velgam Vihara**, Sri Lanka's only Tamil vihara (Buddhist shrine)

In the far north of the district is **Tiriyai Vatadage**, a splendid 7th-century circular Buddhist shrine.

Above: *Pigeon Island is the main habitat of the rare blue rock pigeon.*
Left: *Much of the interior of Trincomalee district is farmland, producing staple crops.*

Travel Tips

The tsunami of Dec 2004 caused the death of over 30,000 Sri Lankans and devastating damage to coastal regions. The east coast saw the highest water levels and loss of life, but damage along all coasts was dependent on local topographical conditions and factors such as the angle of the arriving waves. The island's flora and fauna is recovering well and much of the tourist infrastructure has already been rebuilt. In the east and north, however, where tourism has less of a foothold, recovery is taking longer, while the political situation remains volatile.

A
B
33
C
D
1
2
3
4
5
37
45
N
3000m+
2000-3000m
1000-2000m
500-1000m
200-500m
100-200m
0-100m
INDIAN OCEAN
Kokkuttoduval
Chundikula & Kokkilai Bird Sanctuary
Kokkilai
Tennamaravadi
Kokkilai Lagoon
Pulmoddai
Amarivayal
Eramadu
Yan Oya
Tiriyai
Vatadage of Tiriyai
Kuchchaveli
Eastern Province
Adampane
Pangurugaswewa
Kumpurupiddi
Irrakkakandi
Nilaveli
Tirappanai
Gomarankadawela
Kambakkoddai
Velgam Vihara
Sempadu
Sampaltivu
Dutuwewa
Pankulam
A12
Kanniyai
Uppuveli
Pigeon Island
VAVUNIYA
46
Mora Wewa
Kanniyai Hot Wells
Fort Frederick
Swami Rock (Lover's Leap)
China Bay
Trincomalee
Fort Ostenburg
Naval Headworks Sanctuary
Foul Point
Koddiyar Bay
Tampalakamam
Kinniyai
Vannatidal
North Central Province
Sampur
Ilakkantai
Tamaraivillu
Mutur
Kaddaiparichchan
A6
22
Anaolondawa
Tinneriveli
Malaimuntai
Vendarasan Kulam
Toppur
Palattadichchenai
Dagoba
Kantale Tank
Trincomalee District
Kankuveli
Seruwawila
Ullackale Lagoon
Kantale
Kiliveddi
Allai Tank
Potankadu
Agbopura
Somapura
Ichchilampattai
Kandurukanda 293 m
Somawathie Chaitiya Sanctuary
Sunkankuli
DAMBULLA
VAKARAI

Puttalam District

A long slim district with a vast amount of west coast seafront, Puttalam lies to the north of Colombo. Its close proximity to the war zone meant tourism development concentrated south of the capital, but the miles and miles of sublime sand stretching from the mouth of the Maha Oya in the south all the way up the coast are bound to be one of the dream tropical destinations of the future. In the north the coastline splits from the mainland to make way for Puttalam Lagoon and the district capital Puttalam sits on its eastern bank. This is the heart of coconut and rice production, one of the breadbaskets of staple foodstuffs for the Sri Lankan population.

Above: *Sri Lankan women carry water from the well on their heads, as they have for generations.*
Top left: *Making offerings to the gods is a central precept of the Hindu religion. Here the statue of a god is bathed in fragrant garlands placed by worshippers.*
Left: *Sloth bears are specialist termite eaters, though they also supplement their diet with eggs, fruits, vegetables and honey.*

Main Attractions

Set on its own small inland lagoon, Chilaw was, for generations, a centre for pearl diving. There's a small Dutch fort here but it's famed for the **Munnesvaram Temple**, the most southerly Hindu Shaviate isvarams on Sri Lanka, where the faithful believe that the god Vishnu came to pray. Further north at Udappuwa, the Hindu temple plays host to **fire-walking ceremonies** – known as the Treading of the Flowers – in homage to the goddess Draupadi, wife of the five Pandava heroes. **St Anne's Church** at Talawila out on the coastal spit was founded in the early 18th century, it is said by shipwrecked sailors. At the tip of the peninsula, Kalpitiya has **St Peter's Church** and the ruins of an old Dutch fort. The **coral reef** here has yet to see large numbers of divers. The far north of the district forms the southern sector of **Wilpattu National Park**, the largest in Sri Lanka.

A
B
C
D
35
42
49
1
2
3
4
5
Wilpattu National Park
Puttalam District
North Western Province
Kurunegala District
Puttalam Lagoon
Mundal Lagoon
Tabbowa Wewa
Inginimitiya Reservoir
Rajangana Reservoir
Kala Oya
Mi Oya
Kalagamu Oya
Deduru Oya
ANURADHAPURA
YAPAHUWA
KURUNEGALA
KOCHCHIKADE
A12
A10
A3
60
62
33
31
82
67
58
Kalpitiya
St Peter
Karaitivu
Periyanagavillu
Vannativillu
Nagamadu
Karadipuval
Talawila
Palakkudah
St Anne
Puttalam
Mampuri
Palavi
Madurankuli
Perukkuwattan
Mangalaveli
Mundal
Udappuwa
Kiriyankaliya
Battulu Oya
Anaivilundawa
Rajakadaluwa
Bangadeniya
Chilaw
Dutch Fort
Munnesvaram Temple
Kokkawila
Kakkapalliya
Mahawewa
Kudawewa
Dummalasuriya
Maragahawewa
Nochchiyagama
Kala Oya
Pahala Halmillewa
Puliyankulama
Tumbulagama
Palugassegama
Warawewa
Pahala Giribawa
Kumbukwewa
Galawewa
Tabbowa
Karuwalagaswewa
Sellankandal
Murukkuwatawana
Navagattegama
Tammannawetiya
Kalladi
Mahananneriya
Maha Uswewa
Maha Thorawa
Kollankulama
Kottukachchiya
Tonigala
Dangaswewa
Anamaduwa
Kumbukwewa
Mahakumbukkadawala
Kaluachchigama
Palugaswewa
Timbiriyawa
Andigama
Nikaweratiya
Witikuli
Pallama
Padeniya
Padeniya Vihara
Kobeigane
Torakotuwa
Hettipola
Bingiriya
Bowatta
Panduvasnuwara Citadel
Munamaldeniya
Katupota
Koshena
Udubaddawa
Kuliyapitiya
Dandagamuwa
Kadahapola
N
3000m+
2000-3000m
1000-2000m
500-1000m
200-500m
100-200m
0-100m

A
B
C
D
37
1
2
3
4
5
41
45
50
N
Anuradhapura District
North Western Province
Kurunegala District
Matale District
ANURADHAPURA
Hidogama
Nachchaduwa
Galkulama
Payirimaduwa
Galewewa
Talawa
Nachchaduwa Tank
Turuwila Tank
Tirappane
Yakalla
Padikaramaduwa
Ottappuwa
Kattamurichchan
Hurulu Wewa
Nallamudewa
Angamuwa Tank
Tambuttegama
Eppawala
Ritigala Strict Natural Reserve
World Heritage Site
AGBOPURA
Gal Oya
Gal Oya Junction
Rajangana Reservoir
Maradankadawala
Ritigala 766 m
Madawala
Maha-Iluppallama
Morakanda
Ganewalpola
Medagama
Rajangana
Kunchikulama
Valpotuwewa
Palugaswewa
Mahagalkadawala
Migalawa
POLONNARUWA
Rock Temple
Kalawewa
Kekirawa
Demunnewa
Morgaswewa
Ambagaswewa
Habarana
Sasseruwa Buddha
Minneriya Tank
Kala Wewa
Aukana Buddha
Negampaha
Galgamuwa
Aukana Ancient City
Minneriya Giritale Sanctuary
Balau Wewa
Sigiriya
Siyambalewa
Madatugama
Ehetuwewa
Inamalawa
Kibissa
Citadel of Sigiriya Monolith "Lion Rock"
Galpitagama
Tuttiripitiya
Moragollagama
Andiyagala
Konduruwana
Pelbendiyawa
Mirisgon Oya
Kandalama
Kandalama Tank
Uduweriya
Nikawewa
Dambulla
Attanakadawala
Konwewa
Madagalla
Dambulla Rock Cave Temple
Raja Maha Vihara
Maho
Polpitigama
Yapahuwa
Kottapitiya
Balalla
Yapahuwa Rock Fortress
Kadawala
Alutwegedara
Pannampitiya
Bakamuna
Nagollagama
Welangollo
Galewela
Dambagolla
Elahera
Rambe
Wahakotte
Wasgomuwa Strict Natural Reserve
Naula
Divulwewa
Kongahawela
Kumbukgete
Nalanda Gedige
Ganewatta
Hiripitiya
Madipola
Nalanda
Melsiripura
Kaluganga
Arankele
Mahawela 1233 m
Arankele Ancient Sylvan Monastery
PUTTALAM
Pallepola
Madawela Ulpota
Gokarella
Spice Garden
Mahakeliya
Gammaduwa
Bamunakotuwa
Mahaweia
Kawudupelella
Dodangaslanda
Wellawa
Ibbagamuwa
Dombawela
Maspota
Ridigama
Pallegama
Galgamuwa
Pubbarawela
Ridiviharaya
Guruwela
Palapatwela
Large Rock Outcrops
Rattota
Handapanwela
Aluvihare
Kaikawala
Kurunegala
Barandara
Aluvihare Rock Temple
Uhumiya
Mandandawela
Mallawapitiya
Matale
Ancient Capital
Karagahalande
Kalugamuwa
KANDY
3000m+
2000-3000m
1000-2000m
500-1000m
200-500m
100-200m
0-100m

Matale District

Forming the geographical link between Kandy and the Hill Country to the south and Anuradhapura and the Cultural Triangle to the north, Matale district has its own share of historical, religious and natural attractions. The region was highly populated during both the Anuradhapura and Polonnaruwa capital eras and was a favoured place for the establishment of Buddhist shrines and temples. Craftsmen in Matale town became renowned for their painting and carving - the skills being passed from father to son. Later during the colonial period the land was cultivated with cash crops that made a fortune in Europe. Today it is still the heart of fragrant spice country.

Main Attractions

Matale town is known for its excellent traditional crafts from batik to carving. The market is one of the best places to shop for souvenirs. **Aluvihare Rock Temple** just north of town was first used as a place of worship in the 1st century bc. In fact it is thought that the oral traditions of the faith were first recorded in writing on this site. The caves have many frescoes depicting Buddhist doctrine.

Travelling north, the **Spice Garden** at Kawudupelella is the place to see a range of commercial spices being grown and to find out about their history and their uses.

Dambulla, in the far north, has one of Sri Lanka's finest **cave temples**. Within five large caverns - the largest some 50m (360ft) deep and 6m (19ft) in height - are sitting, standing and reclining Buddha images by the dozen interspersed with shrines to the Hindu gods. Each cave is decorated with scenes from the life of Buddha, though it is worth mentioning that they are much more modern than the statues themselves. The first temples were said to have been created by King Valagam Bahu (104–76BC) of Anuradhapura, who took shelter here after being deposed by southern Indian invaders. On regaining his throne he declared the caves holy land as a means of thanking the gods for sparing his life. **Sigiriya** also sits within the district boundary but has been covered within the attractions of the Cultural Triangle (see page 19).

One of the most interesting temples in Sri Lanka is **Nalanda Gedige**, 20km (12.5 miles) north of Matale. The only large Tantrayana, or Tantric Buddhist temple, it is thought to mark the geographical centre of the island and was one of the earliest stone structures when it was erected in the 8th century.

Above: *Sigiriya Rock is one of the most dramatic palace locations in the world.*
Left: *The Sigiriya frescoes comprise the finest secular art in Sri Lanka.*

Travel Tips

Religious Etiquette
When visiting shrines, temples and mosques remember to dress modestly - no shorts or vests (singlets). Women should cover their shoulders and cover their heads when entering mosques. Take any headgear off when entering a Buddhist temple.

You'll need to leave your shoes at the entrance to a mosque or a Buddhist shrine. In a Buddhist shrine don't point with hands or feet and don't stand with your back to the deity.

Most Buddhist temples will expect a small donation and you should have small change for the guardian of the shoes at a mosque.

Polonnaruwa District

The region surrounding Polonnaruwa, the capital of Sri Lanka (see page 20) during the Middle Ages, is cleaved by the mature path of the Mahaweli Ganga, Sri Lanka's largest watercourse. The river's lazy meandering creates a wide swathe of lush grassland in the heart of the island's dry zone that's a haven for native flora and fauna. Vast tracts of this flood plain were designated protected land, offering extended ranges for large grazing animals and their predators. By contrast, the south of the district is hilly and forested, a favourite playground for the Kings of Polonnaruwa and a repository of medieval religious art and architecture, much of which lies in remote hillside caves.

Main Attractions

North of Polonnaruwa is the 1300-year-old temple site of Mandaligiri Vihara, a circular vatadage with four 8th-century seated Buddha images. The most important site southeast of Polonnaruwa is the pilgrimage site of Dimbulagala with its attendant monastery. Set atop a rocky peak, it is famed for its cave frescoes, the finest of which are still known by the colonial British name - Gunner's Quoin.

One of Sri Lanka's smaller protected sites, the **Minneriya Giritale Sanctuary**, surrounds Minneriya Tank (Reservoir) and offers a rich environment to birds, with over 160 species having been recorded here. Further south, the **Wasgomuwa Strict Natural Reserve** and the **Somawathie Chaitiya Sanctuary** have been linked by a protected jungle corridor along the banks of the Mahaweli Ganga and offer protection to many plains grazers.The ancient Buddhist sanctuary of **Somawathie Dagoba**, the first repository of the sacred tooth of Buddha, is located on the banks of the river.

Travel Tips

Climate
Sri Lanka has two climatic areas - the 'wet zone' in the southwest with over 250cm of annual rainfall and the 'dry zone' in the north and east with 120-190cm of annual rainfall.

Top: *It seems hard to believe that Topa Wewa (Parakrama Samudra) is a man-made lake, but the engineers employed by the Kings of Sri Lanka were highly adept at conserving water and irrigating the land.*
Bottom: *The Audience Hall of the Royal Palace at Polonnaruwa was once one of the most important locations on the island, the venue where the Kings of Sri Lanka met with royal dignitaries and ambassadors of other lands.*

A
B
C
D
39
42
47
53
1
2
3
4
5
N
TRINCOMALEE
A6
Alut Oya
Somawathie Chaitiya Sanctuary
Wadigawewa
Panveli
Migaswewa
Kaudulla Tank
Mandaligiri Vihara
Medirigiriya
Diyasenpura
Talakolawewa
Palliyagodella
Diwulan-kadawala
Somawathie Dagoba
Trikonamadu Natural Reserve
Trikonamadu
Vellai
Verugal
80
Kathiraveli
A15
Vakarai
Panichchankeni
Uppar Lagoon
Kokkavillu
Mankerni
SIGIRIYA
Minneriya
Hingurakgoda
Sungwila
Kandakadu
Minneriya Giritale Sanctuary
41
Tambala
Jayanthipura
Onegama
Mahaweli Ganga
Mutugalla
Polonnaruwa District
65
Punani
Nasuvantivu
Polonnaruwa
Parakrama Samudra
Medieval Capital
Kaduruwela
Welikanda
Maduru Oya
Vakaneri
Trikkandimadu
BATTICALOA
Vakaneri Tank
A11
Kolakanaweli
Ganangolla
Gallella
Mannampitiya
Dimbulagala Monastery
Angamedilla
Amban Ganga
534 m
Dimbulagala (Gunner's Quoin)
Yakkure
Wasgomuwa Strict Natural Reserve
Siripura
Ulpothawewa
Meyankolla
Miyangolle Ela
Aralaganwila
Lavani Aru
Batticaloa District
Bandanagala
Pimburattewa Tank
Dehiattakandiya
44
42
Rukam
Thumpalancholai
Rukam Tank
Mundeni Aru
Ulhitiya Oya
Kudavila
Maduru Oya Reservoir
Pulaveli
Periyapullumalai
Hettipola
Hembarawa
Ratkinda Reservoir
Maha Oya
28
Maduru Oya National Park
A5
Girandurukotte
Ulhitiya Reservoir
BADULLA
3000m+
2000-3000m
1000-2000m
500-1000m
200-500m
100-200m
0-100m

Batticaloa District

Batticaloa, known as Batti to the locals, stands on a long, sandy spit separated from the mainland by a 100km long brackish lagoon that extends southward for many kilometres. In the 1980s, LTTE guerrillas seized control of the town, but were expelled in 1991. Although Batti remained in government hands, the countryside of the district was considered unsafe for travellers until the ceasefire in 2002 and in that time much of the fledgling tourism infrastructure disintegrated. The region remains poor, with fishing the only major industry. This area suffered particularly badly when the tsunami hit and many villages were completely washed away.

Main Attractions

Set at the entrance to the long sinuous lagoon, Batticaloa was one of a string of settlements fortified by the Dutch after it was captured by Admiral Adam Westerwolt in 1638. Unfortunately the town has few historical attractions to hold the visitor.

The lagoon behind the town has long supported a large fishing fleet but the most famous marine species is the 'singing fish,' which can be heard on the moonlit nights between April and September. The sound is said to be a monotone 'vibration' rather than a clear tone – so don't expect Pavarotti!

North of Batti, as the town is known to every Sri Lankan, are stretches of fine sand beach stretching along **Kalkudah Bay,** while to the south are a number of lagoons, all of which are almost wholly undeveloped for tourism. Once the worst ravages of the tsunami have passed and with the peace talks between the rebels and the government progressing, this is one of the world's most interesting and spectacular coastal journeys for more adventurous travellers.

Above: *Sunsets across the lagoon at Batti have an ethereal quality.*
Below: *Fishermen still eke out a living in the lagoon at Batticaloa though the tsunami of 2004 caused major damage to the fleet.*

A
B
C
D
1
2
3
4
5
3000m+
2000-3000m
1000-2000m
500-1000m
200-500m
100-200m
0-100m
N
INDIAN OCEAN
Elephant Point
Vandeloos Bay
45
Passekudah Bay
Kalkudah
Kamburumulai
Kalkudah Bay
Sittandikudi
POLONNARUWA
A15
Chenkaladi
Eravur
A5
Lagoon
23
Batticaloa
Oldest Dutch Settlement
Mantivu
Ayittiyanalai
Kattankudi
Talankuda
F
Unnichchai
Kokkadichcholai
Cheddipalaiyam
Korukkapuliyuttu
Temple
Pulukunavai
Divulanai
47
Paddiruppu
A27
61
Navakiri Aru Tank
Mandur
Bakkiella
AMPARA
SAMMANTURAI
55

Colombo District

Although small by the standards of other country capitals Colombo is still growing at a dramatic rate and the surrounding district bears the brunt of this population pressure. Over 400,000 people make their way into the capital every day for work, and most live close by within commuting distance. The seeds of tourism were first planted close to the capital at the end of the 19th century, and with the arrival of cheaper air travel in the 1970s the beaches just north and south of the city saw the first resort hotels. Today tourism has, for the most part, moved away from the district to better beaches in the southwest and south.

Useful Contacts

Jetwing Eco Holidays - Jetwing House, 46 Navam Mawatha, Colombo 2, tel: (011) 238 1201, fax: (011) 471 4828, www.jetwingeco.com - have over 20 years' experience in eco-tours and wildlife safaris. They can create a package with any theme and include hotels and guides.

Left: *Situated within the cinnamon gardens district, Colombo's largest park becomes a spectacle of colour during springtime, Originally known as Victoria Park, it was renamed Viharamahadevi in the 1950s.*
Below: *Don't be shy to try unusual local fruits like custard apples, jackfruit, mangosteen and rambutan, in addition to the more common tropical fruits.*

Main Attractions

The smallest of Sri Lanka's three botanical gardens, **Henarathgoda** or **Gampaha**, played a crucial role in kick-starting the rubber industry in the British colonies when a cache of 70,000 seedlings smuggled (under conditions of great secrecy) by a British agent from Brazil in the 1870s were grown here before being moved to found plantations across Southeast Asia. The crop became an economic staple of the British Empire well into the 20th century and changed the landscape in many countries from Burma to Malaysia.

The site of **Raja Maha Vihara** is venerated because Lord Buddha shared a meal with the Naga King on the site. Relics of the repast were said to have been buried at the site, sealing the bond between the Holy aura of man and the land on which he had eaten. The Portuguese destroyed the shrine in 1510, but the buildings were resurrected in the 1760s during Dutch suzerainty.

A
B
C
D
41
50
57
1
2
3
4
5
3000m+
2000-3000m
1000-2000m
500-1000m
200-500m
100-200m
0-100m
N
INDIAN OCEAN
CHILAW
Walahapitiya
Marawila
Nattandiya
Dunekedeniya
Yakwila
Narammala
Dampelessa
Dambadeniya
Dambadeniya Tooth Relic
Koswatta
Lunuwila
Katuneriya
Wennappuwa
Coconut Research Institute
Nainamadama
Pannala
Makandura
Giriulla
Dankotuwa
Sandalankawa
Bolawatta
Maha Oya
Alawwa
Kotadeniyawa
Kochchikade
Godigomuwa
Gampaha District
Katana
Mirigama
Ambepussa
Warakapola
Negombo
Dutch Fort
St Mary
Dunagaha
Diwulapitiya
Kota Vihara
Pallewela
Kurana
Katunayake
Minuwangoda
Veyangoda
Pasyala
Negombo Lagoon
Seeduwa
Kotugoda
Udugampola
Nittambuwa
Attanagalla
Pamunugama
Henarathgoda Botanical Gardens
Gampaha
Urapola
Varana
Ja-Ela
Ganemulla
Yakkala
Miriswatta
Gonagalderiya
Kandana
Ragama
Weliweriya
Kirindiwela
Welisara
Henegama
Radawana
Kadawata
Weke
Hendala
Dalugama
Raja Maha Vihara
Pugoda
Royal Colombo Yacht Club
Peliyagoda
Kelaniya
Malwana
Dompe
Avissawella
Kosgama
Kotikawatta
Kaduwela
Kelani Ganga
Puwakpitiya
Palace Berendi Kovil
COLOMBO
Royal Colombo Golf Club
Colombo District
Hanwella
Getahetta
RATNAPURA
Kalatuwawa Reservoir
Waga
Sri Jayewardenepura
Maharagama
Dehiwala-Mount Lavinia
Kottawa
Homagama
Labugama Reservoir
Kahutuduwa
Kesbewa
Handapangoda
Bolgoda Lake
Western Province
Moratuwa
Gonapola
Ceylon Motor Yacht Club
Widiyagoda
Ingiriya
Egoda Uyana
Kalupahana
Nambapana
Panadura
Horana
Kalu Ganga
Alubomulla
Bandaragama
Tuttiripitiya
Egaloya
Gonaduwa
Bulathsinhala
Wadduwa
Kehellenawa
Kalutara District
BERUWALA
KURUNEGALA
A1
A2
A3
A4
A6
A8
A33

A
B
C
D
1
2
3
4
5
42
49
53
59
N
Central Province
Kandy District
Kegalla District
Nuwara Eliya District
Province of Sabaragamuwa
Potuhera
Kurunegala
Mawatagama
Ankumbura
Katupitiya
Weuda
A10
Galagedara
Panwila
Tunhisgala (Knuckles)
1863 m
Looloowatta
Wattegedara
Wattegama
Rangala
Polgahawela
Madawala
Colombo
Rambukkana
Kadigomuwa
Udispattuwa
Pilgrim Museum
Kandy
Dalada Maligawa
Hunnasgiriya
Alagalla
Menikdiwela
Elephant Bathing
Urugalla
Pinnewala Elephant Orphanage
Utuwankanda (Castle Rock)
Royal Botanical Gardens
Kundasale
Medamahanuwara
Victoria Reservoir
Badulla
A19
Balana
Peradeniya
Kegalla
Udamulla
A1
Mawanella
Kadugannawa
Talatu Oya
Victoria Randenigala Rantambe Sanctuary
Galigomuwa
Wattappola
Lankatilake Vihara
Randenigala Reservoir
Batgala
798 m
Bible Rock
Embekke Devale
Dedigama
Hettimulla
Geliyoya
Galaha
Marassana
Archaeological Museum
Kehelwatta
Potgul Magila Vihara
Hemmatagama
Hanguranketa
Pindeniya
Gampola
Deltota
A21
A5
Aranayaka
Rikillagaskada
Undugoda
1118 m
Pupuressa
Pannala
Galapitamada
Bulatkohupitiya
Wathumulla
Salgala
Dedugala
Dolosbage
Ulapane
Maturata
Pussellawa
Kurundu Oya
Kegalla District
Ramboda
Anguruwella
Nawalapitiya
Morape
Ruwanwella
Kotmale Reservoir
Ramboda
Yatiyantota
Belilena
Brookside
Karawanella
Hangran Oya
Kotmale
Pundaluoya
Ragala
A7
Pidurutalagala
2524 m
Kandapola
Kitulgala
Ginigathena
Nuwara Eliya Golf Club
Nuwara Eliya
St Clair
Dehiowita
Aberdeen
Watawala
Watagoda
Kikilimana
2240 m
Galway's Land Sanctuary
Devon
Deraniyagala
Talawakele
Dimbula
Nanu Oya
Hakgala
Laksapana
Rozella
Kotagala
Lindula
Hakgala Botanical Gardens
Hatton
Elgin
Keppetipola
3000m+
2000-3000m
1000-2000m
500-1000m
200-500m
100-200m
0-100m
Maliboda
Dikoya
Agarapatana
Ambewela
Eheliyagoda
Castlereagh Reservoir
Horton Plains National Park
A4
Bopath Ella
Maskeliya
Norwood
Pattipola
Parakaduwa
Sri Pada (Adam's Peak)
2243 m
Bogawantalawa
Ohiya
Pussella
Carney
Maussakelle Reservoir
Kirigalpotta
2395 m
Baker's
Peak Wilderness Sanctuary
Upcot
World's End
Kuruwita
Kalupahana
Idangoda
Bambarakanda
Dodampe
Gilimale
Galagama
Halpe
Kiriella
Gemmological & National Museum
Pinnawala
Kahangama
Gallella
Kadurugalawatta
Belihul Oya
Ratnapura
Samanalawewa Reservoir
Kotamulla
Tiruwanaketiya
Rassagala
Imbulpe
Kirindi Ella
Lellopitiya
Ayagama
Palawela
Balangoda

Kandy District

The ancient highland capital of Kandy is still the true heart of Sri Lanka, where the last Sinhalese kings held out against the European powers, protected by the natural defences of their steep hills and dense tropical forests. The city sits within a loop of Mahaweli Ganga, one of Sri Lanka's more substantial rivers, on the shore of Kandy Lake. Kandy is surrounded by verdant hills that form the breadbasket of the island. Cinnamon and nutmeg plantations scent the breeze and working elephants are still a common sight, toting logs and other loads. Further south, tea is king, and the succulent leaf tips collected here still earn the country millions of dollars each year.

Accommodation

Le Kandyan, Heerasgalla, tel: (081) 223 3521, fax: (081) 223 3948. The Kandy area's newest and most luxurious hotel, in landscaped grounds.
Mahaweli Beach Hotel, 35 PBA Weerakoon Mawatha, PO Box 78, tel/fax: (081) 223 2068. Another luxurious place to stay in the region, with huge outdoor pool and sports facilities.
Helga's Folly, 70 Frederick E Silva Mawatha, tel: (081) 223 4571, www.helgasfolly.com Former family mansion, now an eclectic boutique hotel.
Hotel Tree of Life, Yahalatenna, Werallagama, tel: (081) 249 9777, fax: (081) 249 9711, www.hoteltreeoflife.com Comfortable new hotel offering Ayurvedic health treatments, massage, herbal saunas and aromatherapy.
Hotel Suisse, 30 Sangaraja Mawatha, tel: (081) 223 3024, fax: (081) 223 2083. Good value for money, clean; reasonable facilities.

Above right: *The Temple of the Tooth at Kandy shelters one of the holiest relics of the Buddha in the entire world, and attracts pilgrims from all over Sri Lanka.*

Travel Tips

The **Maha Perahera festival** is held in Kandy in July. This is the largest and most colourful celebration on the island, when the sacred gold 'tooth reliquary' is paraded around the town on the back of the Maligawa Tusker, the largest elephant in Sri Lanka. The festivities last for ten days and nights, climaxing on the sixth day with a vast procession through the streets.
The best time to visit **Pinnewala Elephant Orphanage** is between 10:00 and midday, and 14:00 and 16:00, when the keepers bring their charges down to the river to bathe and play.

Main Attractions

Overlooking Kandy Lake, the **Temple of the Tooth** (Dalada Maligawa) is a place of pilgrimage for millions, and is regarded by Buddhist Sri Lankans as the treasury of their entire culture. The Tooth Relic (tooth of Lord Buddha) itself is claimed to have come to Sri Lanka some 1600 years ago and has been protected in Kandy since around ad1100. The current temple dates from 1687, with additions by a succession of Kandyan kings over the next 95 years.

The **Sri Dalada Museum** houses artefacts used in the daily Tooth Relic ceremonies plus many other religious treasures.
Next to the Temple, the **Kandy National Museum** contains artefacts with a royal civic connection. It was here that the Kandyan chiefs surrendered to the British in 1815.

Trinity College was founded in 1872 to provide education for the children of British administrators and it is still the country's foremost Christian educational establishment. The chapel dating from 1922 is a remarkable blend of western and Sinhalese architectural influences.

About 1km (0.6 miles) east of Trinity College, off Wewelpitiya Road, **Udawattekele** is one of Sri Lanka's more accessible bird sanctuaries, with spectacular parakeets and parrots among the most colourful species.

About 6km (4 miles) southwest of the town, the **Royal Botanical Gardens** at Peradeniya were first planted for King Kirthi Sri Rajasingha (1747–80) and cover some 60ha (150 acres). Under British rule, the royal park became a botanical garden and exotic crops such as coffee, tea, nutmeg, rubber and cinchona (quinine) were tested.

The lush countryside around Kandy is dotted with small Buddhist and Hindu shrines. **Embekke Devale** is a small 14th-century Buddhist temple graced by elaborately sculpted wooden columns. Close by, **Lankatilake Temple** is predominantly a Hindu place of worship but also has Buddhist frescoes. Meanwhile, **Gadaldeniye Temple** is a mainly Buddhist temple with a Hindu shrine attached displaying more 14th-century Buddha images and frescoes.

Badulla District

Lying between the Hill Country to the west and the dryer lower region leading down to the coastal plain to the east, Badulla saw its economic heyday during the later colonial period when it was the westernmost territory of tea country. Badulla town was a leading administrative centre under the British and the terminus for the upcountry railway. A genteel life was to be had, with cricket in the afternoons and gin and tonics in the evenings. Today the region tends to be bypassed by travellers for the delights of Nuwara Eliya (see page 12) higher up in Hill Country, but it's certainly worth adding to the itinerary for its small number of Buddhist temples.

Main Attractions

The primary reason to visit Badulla town today is **Muthiyangana Vihara**, one of the sixteen most venerated Buddhist sites on Sri Lanka. Buddha himself spent some time reflecting at the site and the 4th-century ad shrine houses the Buddha's jawbone. **Dunhinda Falls** (63m/207ft) just outside the town to the north is considered to be the prettiest cascade in Sri Lanka.

South of Badulla, **Bandarawela** was Sri Lanka's first mountain resort when its Bandarawela Hotel opened in 1893. The property, with some additional mod cons, is still open for guests. The **Church of the Ascension** and **Chapel of the Good Shepherd Convent** attest to the strong Christian traditions of the area.

Six kilometres from Bandarawela is **Dowa Cave Temple**, once a sanctuary for King Walagamba. The interior hosts an 11.5m (38ft) sculpture of Buddha sculpted from the living rock, but the intricate entryway is the artistic highlight of the complex.

The southern tank of the **Maduru Oya National Park** dominates the northernmost tip of the district.

Top Right: *Sri Lanka has some dramatic mountain scenery in what has become known as 'the Hill Country'.*
Right: *Tea pickers work hard to pick the crop on the steep slopes of the plantations.*

Travel Tips

Tipping is universal but in modest amounts. A few rupees will be welcomed, especially bearing in mind that many people in coastal settlements lost everything in the 2004 tsunami and need to rebuild their homes and businesses.

A
B
C
D
45
50
55
61
1
2
3
4
5
Ulhitiya Reservoir
Maduru Oya National Park
Kokagala
687 m
MAHA OYA
Serankada
A5
Padiyatalawa
Ellegoda
27
Beligalla
Waywatta
Kehelulla
Holike
Hasalaka
A26
Mahiyangana
KANDY
Raja Vihara
3000m+
2000-3000m
1000-2000m
500-1000m
200-500m
100-200m
0-100m
Ratmalagaha Ella
Namal Oya Reservoir
Mahawala
Weragantota
Ekiriyankumbura
46
Andaulpotha
Kanawegolla
Handaganawa
Victoria Randenigala Rantambe Sanctuary
Minipe
Senanayake Samudra
60
Uraniya
Karamatiya
Radaliyadda
Badulu Oya
Uma Oya
Bibile
Gal Oya National Park
Migahakiula
Arawa
Teripeha
A5
Kanulwela
Yalakumbura
Taldena
Dunedin
Baduluwela
Pallan Oya Tank
Nannapurawa
Badulla District
Madulla
Temple
Buddama
Dunhinda
Lunugala
Medagama
49
45
Muthiyangana Vihara
Province of Uva
Uda Pussellawa
Badulla
47
Kandanketiya
9
Manawela
Magandena
A5
Hali-Ela
15
Ettampitiya
Namunukula
2036 m
Tennugewatta
Dambagalla
Amunekandura
Obbegoda
Galebedda
Welimada
13
Passara
Demodara
Malitta
Nakkala
Kodayana
37
POTTUVIL
Badalkumbura
A22
51
Ella
Namunukula
Monaragala
48
Dowa Cave Temple
Rawana
Wattumbegoda
Hulandawa
Church of the Ascension
21
Ella Gap
Bandarawela
Rawana Ella
25
Kumbukkana
Diyatalawa
A23
Wattegama
Monaragala District
Idalgashinna
A16
A4
Haputale
33
Buttala
Okkampitiya
Beragala
Diyaluma
RATNAPURA
Koslanda
Tarawagama
Maligawila
26
Wellawaya
Habassa
N
Bintenna
723 m
Baduruvagala
Talakolawewa
Mailla
Yala (Ruhuna) National Park
Kumbukkan Oya
A2
HAMBANTOTA

Ampara District

The strangely shaped Ampara district hugs the lower eastern coastline and points a crooked finger into the hinterland towards the Cultural Triangle. This area has a coastline dotted with fishing villages, miles of sandy beaches and some ripping waves for surfers. Inland, vast tracts of land are now protected as national parks, with healthy populations of numerous native species of fauna, including sloth bear, elephant, and the greatest concentration of leopards on Sri Lanka. This was the first section of coastline to be hit by the devastating 2004 tsunami and it took the full brunt of the several pulses of water that traversed the Indian Ocean.

Above: *Many traditional fishing boats were lost in the 2004 tsunami, though the fleet wasn't actually at sea because it was a Hindu holy day.*
Left: *Religion and daily life are totally intertwined in Sri Lanka, where priests are often asked to perform blessings to bestow good fortune or bountiful catches.*
Below Left: *Sri Lanka's wild elephant population have vast tracts of protected land to call home.*

Main Attractions

Surf Mecca, **Arugam Bay** has fantastic beaches and a lagoon where wildfowl flock and elephants come to drink. This is the largest concentration of tourist infrastructure in the district. Inland from the bay and its town, the predominantly Muslim **Pottuvil**, are **Magul Maha Vihara**, built by King Dhatusena in the mid-5th century, though with many 14th-century upgrades, and **Lahugala National Park**, opened in 1980 as part of the wildlife corridor linking **Yala National Park** with Gal **Oya**, where good numbers of elephants and birds gather around the water hole.

In the north, visit **Digavapi Dagoba**, where Lord Buddha is said to have meditated during his second visit to the island in 523BC. A temple was founded on the spot in the 2nd century BC.

Ampara's northwestern corner is dominated by **Maduru Oya National Park**, where there are large populations of primates and several important Buddhist temples dating back to the 6th century BC.

A
B
C
D
47
BATTICALOA
Eastern Province
Andella Oya
Andella Oya Tank
Sorikalmunai
Kalmunai
Chadayantalawa
Sammanturai
Karativu
Nintavur
Uhana
Gal Oya National Park
Malwattai
Pulladiputti
21
A31
A4
Sengapadai
Ampara
Kondavattavan
Digavapi Dagoba
Irakkaman
Irakkaman Tank
Gal Oya
Palamunai
Padagoda
Akkaraipattu
Damana
Periya Kalapuwa
Sinnamuhattuvaram
Ekgal Aru Tank
A25
58
Sakamam Sanctuary
Ambalam Oya Reservoir
Sakamam
Tirrukkovil
Wadinagala
Thottama
53
Ampara District
66
INDIAN OCEAN
Govinda Hela
558 m
Waragoda
Mirahala
Sangamankanda Point
Komari
Lahugala National Park
BADULLA
Magama
A4
35
Siyambalanduwa
Sengamuwa
Lahugala
Pottuvil
Magul Maha Vihara
Arugam Bay
Heda Oya
Raddella
Wila Oya
Panama
Wedagama
Okandawara Bay
Dombagahawela
Wessigewela
Yala East National Park
Okanda
63
3000m+
2000-3000m
1000-2000m
500-1000m
200-500m
100-200m
0-100m
N
1
2
3
4
5

Galle District

The southeast coast hosts some of Sri Lanka's finest tourist resorts and up-market hotel properties, yet there are still miles of uncrowded coastline and the tourist 'explosion' hasn't yet smothered the traditional way of life. From Bentota south, large tropical resort hotels lounge in the shade of coconut palms surrounded by boutiques, beach bars and restaurants interspersed with typical villages with their cluster of family homes. Resort hotels also cluster around Hikkaduwa, and at Koggala, east of Galle. The fine harbour town of Galle, with its UNESCO recognized citadel, anchors the area, with the bulk of the tourist attractions lying close to the golden shoreline.

Main Attractions

The historic town of **Galle** (*see* page 14) with its colonial fortress and bustling commercial centre should not be missed. Strolling around the UNESCO World Heritage site allows for a glimpse of the Sri Lanka of yesteryear.

About 5km (3 miles) south of Bentota, at the fishing hamlet of Kosgoda, is the **Kosgoda Turtle Hatchery**. This charitable organization releases thousands of hatchling green and leatherback turtles into the wild after incubating them in fenced-off areas safe from predators. **Ambalangoda**, 24km (15 miles) south of Beruwala, has a thriving mask and puppet-making industry, making colourful and grotesque *raksha*, *kolam* and *sanni* masks for Sri Lanka's many festivals, processions, and dance-dramas. There's a **private museum** and shop on the main street run by one of the village's noted mask-makers.

About 10km (6 miles) to the south of Ambalangoda, **Hikkaduwa** is the newest and liveliest of the southwest coast beach resorts. There's excellent snorkelling just offshore in the renowned **Coral Gardens** with their vividly colourful reef fish and even the occasional turtle. Just inland from the main coastal highway, 2km (1.5 miles) south of Hikkaduwa, is **Telwatta**, a small lakeside bird sanctuary that offers accessible bird viewing and is especially rich in waterfowl and shore birds.

In the south of the region, **Unawatuna**, less than 5km (3 miles) south of Galle, is a beach resort waiting to happen, while **Koggala** appears in the holiday brochures courtesy of its superb beach. That said, it has plenty to recommend it for an idle, undemanding beach holiday. At **Kataluwa**, 2km (1.2 miles) east of the resort, is a small Buddhist temple worth a visit for its 17th-century frescoes. The long-nosed, vulpine features in European dress are a less than flattering depiction of the Portuguese merchants who ruled the region at the time.

Above: *Relaxing on the as yet uncrowded beach at Unawatuna.*
Top: *The contrasting fishing fleets – small boats for inshore waters and larger boats for the offshore catches.*

Useful Contacts

The website www.lankalibrary.com has a vast amount of useful background information including history, archaeology, heritage and food. There are also some good up-to-date articles on tsunami recovery.

A
B
C
D
49
Kalutara District
1
2
3
4
5
59
Waskaduwa
COLOMBO
Gangatilaka Vihara
Tebuwana
Neboda
Mahagama
Kalutara
Katukurunda
Nagoda
Dodangoda
Pimbura
Agalawatta
Bellana
Lathpandura
Paiyagala
Maggona
Eladuwa
Matugama
Kechchimalai Mosque
Horawala
Beruwala
Kirantidiya
Welipenna
Moragala
Coral Gardens
Dharga Town
Alutgama
Galapata Vihara
Migahatenna
Bentota
Haburugala
Pelawatta
Induruwa
Udugama
Bentota Ganga
Turtle Hatchery
Kosgoda
Pitigala
Uragasmanhandiya
Madu Ganga
Elpitiya
Ahungalla
Kurundugahahetekma
Balapitiya
Dutch Church
Galle District
Ambalangoda
Mask Museum
Batapola
INDIAN OCEAN
Kahawa
Mitiyagoda
Totagamuwa
Baddegama
Gonapinuwala
Hikkaduwa
Coral Gardens
A2
Dodanduwa
Wakwella
Boossa
Gintota
Galle
Dutch Fort
Unawatuna
3000m+
2000-3000m
1000-2000m
500-1000m
200-500m
100-200m
0-100m
N

Matara District

With around 40,000 inhabitants, Matara is the largest town on the south coast and, as the terminus of the railway line from Colombo, the gateway to the region. It's a quiet place, though centuries ago it was one of the most important ports for Sri Lanka's spice and gem trade with the Middle East. It was a strategic port for the Dutch, too, as evidenced by its substantial fortifications. Matara's coastline abuts Galle District to the west but tourism provision is much more low key, with few large hotels and many more family-owned guesthouses. In the aftermath of the tsunami there are plans to alter this balance and rebuild on a grander, more up market scale.

Above: *Statue at the entrance to a temple in Mirissa.*
Left: *Giant Buddha image at Wewurukannala as part of a mythical tableau.*
Below: *The Star Fort at Matara, built in 1763.*

Main Attractions

The oldest part of Matara town sits on a narrow peninsula separated from the mainland by the estuary of the **Nilwala Ganga**, with a good beach on its seaward side. The Dutch encircled this easily defended spit of land with sturdy stone walls. Within the walls is a district of ramshackle old buildings that await renovation and were further damaged by floodwater during the tsunami of 2004. Many date from the Dutch colonial era. Another smaller fort guards the approaches on the opposite riverbank. About 5km (3 miles) east of town is **Dondra Head**, Sri Lanka's southernmost extremity.

On the eastern boundary of Matara district 1.5km (1 mile) north of Dikwella is **Wewurukannala Temple,** with its hundreds of garish life-size models acting out scenes from the life of the Buddha, many-armed devils, monsters and deities, and murals showing the punishments that await sinners in the afterlife (not nice). The courtyard plays host to what's claimed to be the world's highest Buddha image. Built out of reinforced concrete in 1966, it's the height of a five-storey building.

Travel Tips

Matara has an unusual form of urban transportation – carts trimmed with red fabric and drawn by deceptively somnolent looking oxen.

A
B
C
D
50
57
61
1
2
3
4
5
Ratnapura District
Uda Walawe National Park
Uda Walawe Reservoir
Sinharaja Biosphere Reserve
Gongala
1358 m
Haycock
661 m
Southern Province
Matara District
Chandrika Wewa
Koggala Lake
Polwatta Ganga
Nilwala Ganga
INDIAN OCEAN
RATNAPURA
Pelmadulla
Madola
Opanayaka
Rajawaka
Molamure
Mahawalatenna
Diyainna
Dela
Nivitigala
Watapota
Kahawatta
Doloswaka
Karawita
Weligepola
Kalawana
Badureliya
Madampe
Godakawela
Delwala
Delgoda
Weddagala
Rakwana
Pallebedda
Potupitiya
Suriyakanda
Moragoda
Demalagala
Colombage Are
Timbolketiya
Kolonne
Nelluwa
Hayes
Panamure
Embilipitiya
Tawalama
Deniyaya
Hiniduma
Kotapola
Urubokka
Katuwana
Panangala
Morawaka
Waralla
Middeniya
Talgaswela
Kariyamaditta
Pasgoda
Udugama
Rotumba
Nagoda
Dankoluwa
Galpotteyaya
Kurupanawa
Kirama
Pitabeddara
Mawarala
Inanwitiya
Mulatiyana
Walasmulla
Makandura
Wiraketiya
Pahala Vihara Cave Temple
Udayala
Yakkalamulla
Mulgirigala
Kottawa
Akuressa
Kamburupitiya
AMBALANTOTA
Ranna
Hakmana
Henegama
Kirinda
Beliatta
Turtle Conservation Project
GALLE
Angulugaha
Imaduwa
Kananke
Tangalla
Telijjawila
Yatiyana
Wewurukannala Vihara
Hawatuna
Thalpe
Kataluwa Temple
Tihagoda
Palapota
Malimmada
Folk Art Museum
Kustaraja Rock Carving
Aparekka
Habaraduwa
Koggala
Denipitiya
Blowhole
Ahangama
Weligama
Museum of Ancient Paintings
Dikwella
Stilt Fishermen
Mirissa
Matara
Kottegoda
Taprobane (Galduwa Rock Island)
Gandara
Kamburugamuwa
Dutch Fort
Dondra
Dondra Head
A4
A18
A17
A24
A2
8
11
12
19
21
24
28
34
37
48
52
55
56
57
58
59
73
79
N
3000m+
2000-3000m
1000-2000m
500-1000m
200-500m
100-200m
0-100m

Hambantota District

Hambantota, 240km (150 miles) from Colombo, is an independent travellers' haven that is showing some signs of escalating into a fully-fledged holiday resort. Like other south coast towns and villages, it would probably already have made the transition if not for the troubles of the 1980s and 1990s. The whole coastline is characterized by sweeping sandy bays, while inland vast tracts of pristine landscape offer precious environments for a wide range of Sri Lankan flora and fauna. The town is the most convenient base for exploring the district, including nearby Bundala National Park and the Yala (Ruhuna) National Park and the important temple complex at Kataragama.

Main Attractions

Standing on a sandy headland, sleepy Hambantota is a major fishing centre. Just east of the town are a series of saltpans that attract large numbers of waders and shore birds, including greater flamingo and the spot-billed pelican.

East of Hambantota, **Bundala National Park** is a relatively small park but its high concentrations of mammal and bird species make it one of the best places to see Sri Lanka's abundant wildlife. The beaches are egg-laying sites for Olive Ridley and leatherback turtles. Offshore, the **Great Basses reef**, about 40km (25 miles) east of Hambantota, and the **Little Basses**, 80km (50 miles) east, are reputed to offer the best diving in Sri Lanka, with numerous wrecks and fish.

The small town of **Tissamaharama** or Tissa, northeast of Hambantota, is closest to **Ruhuna Yala National Park** (*see* page 62), to the east, and the **Kataragama temple complex**. Tissa was capital of the ancient kingdom of Ruhuna, and its founder, Yatalatissa, built the enormous tank in the centre of town some 2300 years ago.

The **Kataragama shrine** on the banks of a holy river, the **Menik Ganga**, is important to both Buddhists and Hindus. Lord Buddha planted a sapling of the Sacred Bo Tree of Anuradhapura here, sanctifying the spot, while to Hindus it is the dwelling place of Skanda, the Hindu war god. The most important Buddhist shrine, the **Kirivehera Dagoba**, was first erected in the 1st century BC. **Hindu Maha Devala** is said to contain the spear of the multi-visaged, 12-armed warrior deity.

West of the small resort of Tangalla is a **Turtle Conservation Centre**. At **Mulgirigala**, 16km (10 miles) north of Tangalla, a cave temple in a monolithic rock contains statues of Buddha and a series of wall paintings.

Travel Tips

During the **Thaipusam Festival** devout celebrants allow metal skewers to be driven through cheeks and tongues and fire-walkers cross beds of glowing coals.

Above: *Outrigger canoes pulled up out of reach of the surf at Hambantota Beach.*
Below: *Sri Lanka's traditional dances include religious elements and are characterized by lavish costumes and ritualized movements. The themes often revolve around the never ending struggle between good and evil.*

A
B
C
D
BADULLA
53
Telulla
A2
Hambegamuwa
Kuda Oya
59
Galge
Yala (Ruhuna) National Park
1
2
3
4
5
Angunakolapelessa
Nikawewa
Bodagama
Tanamalwila
Kataragama Pilgrim Site
Menik Ganga
Kataragama
Lunuganwehera Reservoir
Wedahitikanda (Kataragama Peak)
424 m
Sithulpahuwa
Katagamuwa
Sithulpahuwa
Yala
Migahajandura
Wirawila Tissa Bird Sanctuary
Lunuganwehera
Suriyawewa
Buthawa
Hambantota District
Pannegamuwa
Tanjanagaram
Yoda Wewa
Debarawewa
Tissamaharama
Malala Oya
Badagiriya
Monolith
Palatupana
63
Gannoruwa
Keliyawalana
Wirawila
54
A18
Siyambalagoda
Karambagala
Uduwila
Kirinda
Ridiyagama Tank
Weligatta
Bundala
Ridiyagama
27
Bundala National Park
Great Basses
Beragama
Godayaya
Girihanda Vihara
18
MATARA
Hambantota
Ambalantota
Nonagama
Hungama
ahandamodara
N
INDIAN OCEAN
3000m+
2000-3000m
1000-2000m
500-1000m
200-500m
100-200m
0-100m

Around Yala National Park

Sri Lanka's most popular national park, Ruhuna, known to everyone as Yala, is easily accessible from Colombo on the A2 coastal highway; the park entrance is about 70km (45 miles) east of Hambantota and 30km (19 miles) east of Tissa. Covering almost 1000km² (386 sq miles) in total, the park comprises scrub jungle, open savannah, riverine woodland and a long coastline of mangrove and beach that curves around Sri Lanka's southeast coast. Yala was a regular venue for 19th-century colonial hunters who shot thousands of the region's elephant and leopard, but this is still the easiest place on the island to enjoy large wild mammals in their native environment.

Main Attractions

Much of the park is the animals' private domain and only the southwest segment, an area of some 130km² (50 sq miles), is open to visitors. **Elephant** get top billing and are what most people come to see. Family groups, led by mature matriarchs, wander uninhibited using their trunks to reach high into the treetops for juicy leaves or to probe the ground for roots.

Other mammals include **sloth bear**, **spotted deer**, **mouse deer**, **barking deer**, **sambur**, **grey langur**, **toque monkey**, **wild boar**, and smaller species including **stripe-necked** and **ruddy mongoose** and **jackal**. Both marsh and estuarine **crocodiles** may be seen, and a day's birding can record as many as 100 species, among them such rarities as **red-faced malkoha**, **great thick-knee**, **sirkeer malkoha**, **blue-faced malkoha** and **painted stork**.

The best place to see a range of animals is around water sources. The **Kumbukkan Oya** and **Menik Ganga** flow through the park. You may see elephant, wild pig, deer, monkeys and even the elusive **pangolin** drinking from the same pool, along with conspicuously colourful **peacock** and jungle fowl.

Access is by vehicle only, and four-wheel drive is required. Ruhuna is usually closed from late August to mid-October. The best time to be sure of seeing the maximum is during the dry season when animals have to share water sources.

Travel Tips

Malaria, **dengue fever** and **rabies** are all endemic to Sri Lanka and the wild areas of the national parks are particular areas of concern. Before travelling to Sri Lanka take advice on updating your inoculations and about suitable malaria prophylaxis. On the ground wear long-sleeved tops and long trousers to avoid mosquito bites, stay clear of animals and keep any cuts or open sores clean.

Pack Imodium or a similar preparation to alleviate symptoms of diarrhoea, as well as electrolyte mix for rehydration. Sunburn and heat exhaustion are significant risks at all times of year and children, especially, should be kept out of the sun as much as possible.

Useful Contacts

With the **Kulu Safari Company** - 6 Alfred House Road, Colombo 3, tel: (011) 259 9450, fax: (011) 250 1287, www.kulusafaris.com – you can enjoy a true safari experience while spending evenings in the comfort of a five-star tented village with hot showers, a comfortable bed, cocktails and sumptuous dinner. Kulu offers trips to Yala and most other Sri Lankan national parks.

Top: *Wild water buffalo can be seen in many lowland national parks. Their domesticated cousins are still in service on the island to tend fields and pull carts.*
Right: *Watching wild elephant playing contentedly in their natural environment is one of the most awe-inspiring activities in Sri Lanka. Elephant families here are well-established offering new arrivals the chance to grow up in a socially stable environment.*

A
B
C
D
1
2
3
4
5
55
61
Yala East
National Park
Kumana Bird
Sanctuary
Mahawelatota
Kirigalla Bay
Kumana
Pothana Bay
Ruhuna Wildlife
Sanctuary
Little Basses
INDIAN OCEAN
N
3000m+
2000-3000m
1000-2000m
500-1000m
200-500m
100-200m
0-100m

TOURIST AREA AND TEXT INDEX

Note: numbers in **bold** denote photographs

MAIN MAP INDEX